One Of The Whosoevers

To: My Long Time
Friend and Fellow
Proclaimer —
Dr. Bertrand M. Bailey Sr.
"The God We Serve
Is Truly Able."
D.H. Colin Macutchen Jr.
03-03-09

One Of The Whoso

The Life Story and A Collection of Sermons

Dr. G. Calvin McCutchen, Sr.

iUniverse, Inc.
New York Lincoln Shanghai

One Of The Whosoevers
The Life Story and A Collection of Sermons

iUniverse books may be ordered through booksellers or by contacting:

iUniverse
2021 Pine Lake Road, Suite 100
Lincoln, NE 68512
www.iuniverse.com
1-800-Authors (1-800-288-4677)

Because of the dynamic nature of the Internet, any Web addresses or links contained in this book may have changed since publication and may no longer be valid.

The views expressed in this work are solely those of the author and do not necessarily reflect the views of the publisher, and the publisher hereby disclaims any responsibility for them.

Life Story Compiled & Edited by Jessie M. Delt

ISBN: 978-0-595-46452-4 (pbk)
ISBN: 978-0-595-70224-4 (cloth)
ISBN: 978-0-595-90749-6 (ebk)

Printed in the United States of America

".... that whosoever believeth in Him should not perish, but have everlasting life."

—Sermons by—

DR. G. C. McCutchen, Sr.

To my wife Adelene
To my son George, Jr.
To my friends

Contents

Introduction

"One Of The Whosoevers" tells the story of a youngster growing up in the hills of Kentucky, who from a very young age had only dreams and aspirations of being a Minister of the Gospel. He went from these humble beginnings with this one desire in his heart, and has gone forth with God to become an honored leader in the nation.

Having been awarded his Doctorate of Divinity degree from the Jackson Theological Seminary—Shorter College, Little Rock, Arkansas; and a Doctorate of Humane Letters from Tennessee Baptist College, Memphis, Tennessee; Dr. George Calvin McCutchen, Sr., has served as Pastor of the Mt. Zion Baptist Church, Tulsa, Oklahoma for the past fifty years. His ministry is filled with seeking new converts, finding fulfillment in the Lord, and preaching so that the kingdom of God might be advanced and enriched.

He gives of himself relentlessly. He tries to help solve problems, soothe sorrows, assuage cares, as well as lead the sinner into a beautiful conversion. He has received many honors and acquired much acclaim from his peers and people in his community, the state, and the nation because of the inspiring messages that he had delivered since accepting the call to the ministry, yet he remains a humble servant for the Lord.

The words that fall upon the waiting hearts of the listening congregation are anointed with Devine power and strength. They bring hope, encouragement, and transformation to all who grasp them as they come forth from the mighty heart of this man of God.

In deliverance of his messages, Dr. McCutchen has a style of putting himself, his testimony, and his experience into the message, which give greater inspiration to those hearing the Word.

This collection of favorite sermons, as written and delivered by Dr. McCutchen, intertwined with his life story, is designed to give the reader the same strengths, inspiration, and encouragement as it has given those fortunate enough to hear his messages in person.

CHAPTER I

"Trust in the Lord with all thine heart and lean not unto thine own understanding. In all thy ways acknowledge Him, and He shall direct thy paths."

(Proverbs 3:5-6)

Born March 1, 1927, black and poor in Warren County, Salem Community, Rockfield, Kentucky, he was expected to grow up to be a farmer. The fifth child of seven children born to William H. and Rosetta Barnett McCutchen, George Calvin was brought up in a three room log cabin located on a five and a half acre farm which had been given to his father from his father.

Many people lived in that community—some lived along Petros Road, where the McCutchen house was situated, others lived in fields where there were no roads—only paths—to be traveled to their house.

"The home I grew up in had none of the modern conveniences we have in homes today. We brought water for drinking, cooking and bathing from a spring that was possibly a quarter of a mile from where we lived. Others who lived in the vicinity got their water from the same source. The spring was a meeting place for many of us as children and youth, because we took our buckets, sometimes our tubs, and made the trip to the spring at least twice a day—mornings and evenings."

The food was cooked on a wood burning stove; the house was warmed by an open fireplace; windows and doors were kept open during summer months while the family slept, because there was no cooling system for the home.

William H. McCutchen was a *share-cropper* who worked for and in the W.P.A. This was a work program made possible through the efforts of President Franklin Delano Roosevelt. Rosetta McCutchen was a housewife, who took care of the home and children, and made a little money doing laundry for the more affluent farmers.

> *"Often I have said we were so poor that the poor folk called us 'Po'. Now that I think about it, we weren't poor at all. We just didn't have any money. We had each other. If we didn't get what we wanted, we wanted what we got."*

On that small farm they had many chickens, a cow and a dog. Prayerfully each year the family raised a good garden with a hoe, asking the Lord to provide the sunshine and rain, and they would keep the weeds chopped out.

When school was not in session, young George Calvin McCutchen learned to do all kinds of work, especially work on the farm. He learned how to walk following a plow. Corn and tobacco were the main crops for that area, so he learned how to work with these crops.

But being a farmer was not the dream or aspiration that filled the mind and heart of young George Calvin McCutchen. For as a child, he had the desire and felt the calling to be a minister of the gospel. His spiritual journey began at a one room country church called Salem Baptist, located on Rural Route 2, Rockfield, Kentucky.

> *"I rejoice now in the fact that our parents did not just tell us about that little church beside the road, they led us there for Sunday School each Sunday, and we stayed for the preaching service each third Sunday."*

In that little wooden church located on Browning Road, as a child, George heard nothing but old fashion Gospel preaching. Many days he heard the preacher say *"Sin is black—hell is hot—Heaven is happy—salvation is free".*

That church did not have a piano or a choir stand. Deacons led in the singing. They kept the time of the song by the clapping of their hands and the patting of their feet. Many times, when they got near the church, the people would hear the singing and get in a hurry because the church had already started.

> *"I was 10 years old when I got saved. I had attended the Revival and was on the mourner's bench for the second year. I was expecting some spectacular emotional experience. It was during a period of revival during the school day, when the minister did not cause us to bow our heads, but to sit up and hear him explain the plan of Salvation. When the plan was properly explained to me I made the most important decision of my life. I decided to follow Jesus."*

The "ministry" was not looked upon as a good occupation in this little community. Most of the Black ministers in the area were untutored, poor, and had little respect.

> *"But I couldn't help it, all I wanted to be was a minister. It was not my own doing. The Lord put me in the ministry."*

Mrs. Ida Nell Finch, his elementary school teacher, encouraged him and taught him to have respect for his dreams. She encouraged him to reach for the higher things in life. She took young George to larger towns so he could hear more skilled, tutored and educated ministers. She told him—*"Calvin, if the Lord has called you, you be proud of that and you stick with it. You stand by your convictions and you be the best minister that you can be."*

The first school young George attended was a one-room school building located in the community about half a mile from his home. His first teacher commuted twelve miles daily from Bowling Green to teach all eight grades housed in that one room building. George attended that school for seven years, graduating one year before time, because he completed the Eight Grade work during his seventh year.

George Calvin attended his first year of high school at Delafield High School in Bowling Green, Kentucky. This was an all black school with only two teachers. Mr. Poole was Principal and taught Algebra, Geometry, and Business Arithmetic. Mrs. Cole taught Social Studies,

English, and Music. The school did not have a dining room, library, or athletic program. At lunch time, the students were excused to go to the nearby grocery store for snacks. The school did have a playground with a basketball court.

The county hired a member of the community to drive the school bus that would pick up the students in the community and drive them into Bowling Green for school. During his third year of high school, George rode the same bus and attended State Street High School. State Street High had three stories and teachers for almost every subject. It was a school for the black students of the city and the rural community.

> *"My goal was to attain a high school education. Not too many, including my mother and father, in the community could boast of having a high school diploma. I was determined to get one someway, and somehow."*

During the summer prior to the beginning of George's senior year in the fall, he learned that the school bus would not be coming to his community for one or two students—ten was the minimum. He made up his mind that he was going to finish high school if he had to hitch a ride to the city each day.

Young George worked for a farmer during that summer who tried to get him to ditch the idea of a high school education. The farmer wanted and needed George to work on the farm, for which he was paid Three Dollars ($3.00) a week plus room and board. He would spend the week at the Mobley Farm and return home on the weekends.

One weekend when George returned home, he found his father, William, to be very ill. His mother had died when he was ten years old; his older sisters were out of the home; his oldest brother, J. W. was already in the Army; Carlyle was working the job his father had; and his two younger sisters were living with his grandmother. George was selected to stay home and take care of his father the best he could. Aunt Lizzie, his father's sister, lived in the community and came to cook and help. His father passed away that summer.

His oldest sister, Esella Zenely, knew of his desire to finish high school and suggested that he get all of his possessions, which were few, and come to Cincinnati, Ohio and live with her until he finished high school. This he did, and enrolled in Woodward High School, located on Sycamore and Cutter Street, downtown Cincinnati. This was an integrated school, the largest George had ever seen in his life, and was within walking distance of where he lived—twenty blocks.

George took a job at a grocery store one block from his home, where he was paid Ten Dollars ($10.00) per week. From that salary, he paid $1.00 in Tithes; took $4.00 for his weekly allowance; and gave $5.00 to his sister who purchased his clothing and gave him room and board.

> *"There were 540 students who graduated in that class of 1944. Woodward High's motto I recall was written in Latin—__Esse quam veder__" translated means—__To be rather than seem__". This motto was engraved on my class ring that I wore for many years."*

George Calvin McCutchen acknowledged his calling to the ministry in the fall of 1944 at age 17, the same year he finished Woodward High School in Cincinnati, Ohio, and preached his initial sermon during the Evening Worship service at Calvary Baptist Church in Cincinnati, on the first Sunday, May 3, 1945. Apparently, George did not make much of an impression upon his pastor, the Reverend E. E. Kelley, during his initial sermon. Reverend Kelley allowed him to go from Cincinnati, Ohio to Louisville, Kentucky without granting him a license to preach.

He remained in Cincinnati about three months after graduating from high school, and moved to Louisville, Kentucky to live with his Aunt and Uncle—Alzie and Mitchell St. Claire.

He took a job in Louisville at the Seagrams Distillery where his Uncle Mitch worked, as a cafeteria worker, and—determined to continue his education—George enrolled in night classes at Simmons Bible College. He attended classes there two nights a week, studying under the late Dr. Jessie Bottoms, who taught Theology, and G. A. Hampton, who taught English and World Literature.

During his first year at the school, George was asked to deliver the welcome speech for a "*Minister's Seminar*" which was being conducted on the campus. In the audience of that meeting was the Assistant Pastor from his home church, Calvary Baptist of Cincinnati. After he heard young George speak, he invited him to come to Cincinnati that weekend to deliver an initial sermon.

When George informed him that he had already delivered his initial sermon at Calvary, but had not received his license, the Assistant said, "*Come home anyway. I'll pick up a license and see that you have it this weekend.*"

His preaching career began shortly thereafter. But, in March 1945 young McCutchen turned 18 and, like all able bodied young men of that time, he received a special invitation from Uncle Sam to join the United States Armed Forces. His calling to the ministry had to be put on hold as a more immediate call from the military draft had to be answered.

In the sign up center there were areas labeled for each branch of the service. Since he had been drafted and had to join one of the branches, George decided that he would join the Army and proceeded in that line to enlist. The line was long and, before he could make it to the sign up table, the heading of the line changed from ARMY to NAVY.

George was very disgusted. He didn't want to join the Navy. He didn't even like their uniforms, in particular those bell bottom trousers and the cap or hat they wore. About that time, the Marines were asking for volunteers. George liked their uniforms, so he volunteered for the U.S. Marine Corp, which he soon learned was the toughest branch of the services.

During this time in young George's life, he almost gave up the idea of becoming a minister; but, he soon found a "buddy" in the Marines who was also a young minister. His platoon sergeant also sensed something different about George and instructed him to have prayer with the other fellows in the unit before bedtime.

George spent two years in the Marines, stationed at Monford Point, Camp Legume, North Carolina, and a few days at Camp Pendleton, San Diego, California, in route to Guam and Siapan. In 1947 he was honorably discharged at the Naval Base in Great Lake, Illinois; and returned to Cincinnati and later to Nashville, Tennessee, where he enrolled at the American Baptist College of the Bible.

He graduated from ABCB in 1950 with a Bachelor of Theology, and that same year enrolled at Tennessee State University, where he majored in History with a minor in English and Sociology.

MY LIFE NEEDS A CAPTAIN
Scripture: Luke 24:1-15

".... Jesus Himself drew near and went with them."

Luke 24:15

It was a spring night and two men were walking the Emmaus Road. They were sadden by their Master's death, and bowed beneath that load. Suddenly another overtakes them as they walk. A stranger falls in step with them and earnestly they talk of what is in their hearts.

Moved by a warm soul stirring glow, they reach their destination and do not wish to let Him go, and so they bid Him stay awhile and share their simple board. As He breaks the bread, they know—they know that He is the Lord.

Jesus never sends a man ahead alone. He blazes a trail and clears the way through every thicket and woods, and then softly calls, *"Follow me. Let us go on together, you and I."*

He has been every where that you and I are "called" to go. His feet have trodden down smooth a path through every experience that comes to us. He knows each road, and He knows them well.

The valleys of disappointments with its dark shadows; the steep paths of temptations; down through the rocky ravines and the slippery gullies; the narrow path of pain with the brambly thorn bushes, so close on each side with tier slash and sting; the dizzy roads along the heights of victory; and the old beaten down path of common place daily routine; all of these everyday roads He has trodden and glorified, and will walk on them anew with each of us.

The only safe way to travel is with Him by your side, and He having complete control. I believe the men that we are talking about today knew such a man—"*.... and Jesus drew near and went with them.*"

He was their companion, their company keeper, and I think they took Him to be the captain of their lives. The one of whom we speak was the Christ of the common folk, for they heard Him gladly.

Where He found fear in the heart of a friend, He left confidence. Where there was bitterness, He brought understanding. Where there was doubt, He planted faith. Where there was felt suspicion, He planted trust. Where there was chaos, God's spirit working within Him helped to bring order. Where there was felt superiority, the quality of His life suggested humility.

I can imagine that George Washington Carver, Booker T. Washington, and Martin Luther King took Him for the Captain of their lives, and I am saying today that My Life Needs A Captain.

I.   **I Need Someone Interested In My General Welfare**

My life needs a Captain, because I need someone who will be interested in my general welfare.

There are many things that face Black people today. We need better job opportunities. We don't need to ride in the rear of buses. We need not be deprived of our many rights as citizens, but many times we are.

We have come a long way, but we still have a long way to go. Between our heartaches and our loved ones, with only a little sunshine every now and then, and the mountains in this life that are so hard to climb, we need someone to give an answer to the many problems we face. Yes! We need someone who is interested in our general welfare.

II.   **I Am Unable To Understand The Mysteries Of Life**

My life needs a captain because I am unable to understand the mysteries of life. It is a mystery to me how the wicked seem to prosper and the righteous seem to suffer so much.

We wonder why men fail to love when Jesus admonished us to love our neighbor as ourselves. Dr. Carver, Booker T. Washington, and Martin Luther King—they learned to love.

In our weaker moments we wonder why God permits so much evil to go on in the world. And so, <u>My Life Needs A Captain</u>— someone that will help me to understand the mysteries of life.

III. I Am Unable To Bear Burdens Alone

My life needs a Captain because I am unable to bear these burdens alone. Young people today do not have the burdens to bear as Dr. Carver, and Booker T. Washington had; nor do they have the burdens that Martin Luther King must bear. They do not have as many burdens that you and I had to bear; but, they do have burdens.

In the olden days the thought of going to high school was a burden unless you had the desire from within. You had to walk long distances and buy your own books. You would start out with a class and very few would make it to the end.

Young people today are faced with the burdens of drugs, peer pressures, violence, etc. But, the good news is they can make it with the right captain of their lives. Thanks be to God I made it. I took the Master along with me because I was unable to bear my burdens alone.

What is a captain in the literal sense? There are many types of captains, but the one I have in mind is that commissioned officer commanding a squadron of ships. I have chosen him because I like to picture the lives of men as ships set assail on a stormy, restless sea.

There are many types of ships, but I will only have time to name three—the canoe, the yacht, and the battleship.

The **Canoe** is man's earliest development as a ship. It has rather a simple construction. Man made it by hewing out a log in the center and giving it a pointed shape at each end. Many a person's life is just like that. A simple construction hewed out in the center and pointed at each end. No one can tell them a thing. They go through life with the bear necessities of things spiritual, and the bear necessities of education. His life was not like a canoe. I ask you today—is your life a canoe.

Then we mentioned the **Yacht** which is a pleasure boat. Are you a person that goes aimlessly through life seeking only the pleasure you can derive there from? Is your life a pleasure boat? If so, it would be better for you that a millstone be hanged about your neck and you be cast into the depth of the sea.

But of all the ships that sail the several seas, I would prefer to be the **Battleship.** Perhaps you wonder why I have chosen the battleship seeing that it is used for the destructive purpose of life. I can see the Christian life with the ruggedness of a battleship plowing the mighty waters that flow from Emanuel's veins, spilling its blood on the robes of sinful men making them white as snow.

In closing, let me leave this thought with you as you go forth into this new year. Like Dr. Carver, Booker T. Washington, and Dr. King—carry with you a compass of standards. Something that will tell you what is right and what is wrong. It is said that they heard their mothers pray; and they never forgot the prayers.

History tells us that Columbus set sail in three small vessels on an uncharted and trackless sea. He was sailing westward day after day, facing the storms without any sight of land, and their supplies were running low. The worried crewmen cried out—"What shall we do? What shall we do?"

Columbus' reply was—"Sail on! Sail on! Sail on!"

I say to you today—whatever be your lot this year, regardless of the consequences, SAIL ON! SAIL ON! SAIL ON!

MISTAKEN TEARS
Scripture: Luke 23:26-31

"... Daughters of Jerusalem, weep not for me, but for yourselves and your children."

Luke 23:28

If there had ever been a just cause for tears, certainly this seemed to have been the time. Three men are headed up a hill to be executed, each carrying their own cross. The crowd, for the most part, seems to be more hostile toward Jesus. They find it easy to ridicule and insult a man who falls beneath his load. But while the people who marched along the road with him, for the most part, are very unfriendly, there are a few exceptions. There are a few women who feel sorry for this man who is being led to such an untimely death. Knowing that he was so innocent and so young, their sorrow for him made them burst into tears.

But the reaction of Jesus to those tears is a bit surprising: for He seems to have no appreciation for their sympathy at all, for He looked toward them and said—"... *Daughters of Jerusalem, weep not for me, but rather weep for yourselves and your children."*

I believe there are two reasons Jesus made this statement. First—I believe that Jesus had a strong man's natural aversion to being pitied. And the second reason He does not appreciate the women's tears is because He sees that they have missed the real point of the tragedy. Theirs are Mistaken Tears.

There are some folk who have no sense of humor, and they laugh not at all. Then there are some folk who have a perverted sense of humor, and they laugh at the wrong things and in the wrong places. Even so, there are those who do not know when or for what reason to weep.

These women were perfectly right in shedding tears, but they were weeping for the wrong cause. Themselves and their children that was the cause of His death. Without Jesus dying on the cross, we would be left alone in a world of sin and sorrow. The same thing that is happening to Him will happen to you.

They stood around there crying for Jesus, when the truth of the matter was, they should have been weeping over themselves and their children. But turning unto them He said—"... *Daughters of Jerusalem, weep not for me, but rather weep for yourselves and your children."*

Jesus was saying to them in so many words that he was not to be pitied, but rather congratulated; and theirs were Mistaken Tears.

So now I'm asking you to pull up a chair and listen; for I have stopped by on my way to Heaven to tell you why we have mistaken tears, and why Jesus should be congratulated.

I.   **His Actions Were In Keeping With The Will Of God.**

First of all, Jesus was to be congratulated because His actions were in keeping with the will of God. His only desire, all through His life, was to do His Father's will. This was an answer to His prayer. Therefore, as He goes up that lonely way, He is conscious that He is right with God and subsequently right with himself. Obeying God, He is enjoying fellowship with God. Hear Him saying.... *"He that hath sent me, is with me."*

This experience was costing Him everything, even His life; He is not to be pitied, but congratulated. No man is suppose to be pitied who is conscious of the fact that he is doing right, he is suppose to be congratulated.

So, I am saying that Jesus was not to be pitied, but congratulated because He was engaged in doing God's will, and theirs were <u>Mistaken Tears</u>.

II.   **He Was Dong The Thing He Had Longed To Do.**

Secondly, Jesus thought himself worthy of congratulations because He was doing the thing He had longed to do.

Those weak hearted women were thinking that the cross was being forced upon His weak shoulders. They were thinking that His rich life was being wrenched out of His hands. But Jesus is saying to them.... I do not have to bear this cross, I am doing it because of my own choice; I am not losing my life, I am giving it; no man takes my life, I am laying it down for myself; I have found something in this world big enough to live for. Yea! And big enough to die for. Therefore, don't weep over me, but congratulate me.

The real joyous folk are those who take upon themselves the burdens that nobody has the right to ask them to carry. To weep over them, is to shed <u>Mistaken Tears</u>.

So, I am saying that Jesus is to be congratulated rather than pitied because He is doing what He mostly wanted to do.

III.　**He Is Living Victoriously**

Note next that Jesus is to be congratulated rather than pitied because He is living victoriously. If there was ever a man that seemed to have been defeated, it was Jesus. At one time He was very popular. Great multitudes thronged His every step. But now His popularity has changed to hot hatred and bitter antagonism. And, from the surface, it looks now like He is a pathetic failure.

But, He is not defeated, He is living victoriously. For just a few hours before He had told His disciples.... *"In this world ye shall have tribulations. But be of good cheer, I have overcome the world."*

So, I am saying that Jesus needed to be congratulated rather than pitied because He was living a victorious life.

IV.　**He Was Practicing What He Preached**

Note next that Jesus was to be congratulated because He was practicing what He preached. What He had preached on the mountain, He was being given an opportunity to practice on the mountain. He had preached forgiveness, and now He was being given the opportunity to forgive His enemies. Hear Him in His final words— *"Father, forgive them for they know not what they do."*

He had preached that man must go the second mile and must turn the other cheek; here He was given the opportunity to prove that it could be done.

So, I am saying that Jesus should have been congratulated rather than pitied because He was practicing what He had preached; and, to weep over a man who is practicing what he preached is to shed stupid and <u>Mistaken Tears</u>.

V.　**He Was Dying That Men Might Live**

Many years ago all along the country roads you could find the little flour mills. It was in one of these mills that a little child was playing. He was playing close to the machinery—he had no business there and he knew it—but you know how children are prone to disobey.

Well this is what happened. His clothing got caught into the machinery and he was being drawn closer and closer to an untimely death. There was a Negro working there in the mill and saw what was happening. He didn't have time to run to the switch and shut off the machinery. He knew that the only thing for him to do was jam the machinery. But looking quickly around him, he couldn't find anything to stop the wheel; so he deliberately put his elbow into the wheel and caused the machinery to stop. The poor man's arm was so mangled that he had to have it removed. And, from the pain and the lost of blood, he went on to meet his maker. That child never did forget that. A man died that he might live.

That is what Jesus was doing for all of us. We were like disobedient children; playing around the machinery of the world. Our clothes caught in the wheels and we were being drawn closer and closer to an endless death. But Jesus stopped the wheels of the machinery from turning when he went to Calvary and laid down His life that we might live.

It was alone—all alone—He bore it all alone. He gave Himself to save His own. He suffered, bled and died—alone.

He was to be congratulated rather than pitied because He was giving up His life that we might live. To weep over Him in that redemption hour was to be shedding stupid and <u>Mistaken Tears</u>.

THE TRAGEDY OF LEAVING JESUS ON THE OUTSIDE OF YOUR LIFE
Scripture: Revelations 3:12-26

"Behold, I stand at the door and knock; if any man will hear My voice and open the door, I will come in and sup with him and he with me."

Revelations 3:20

A tragedy is a mournful event that has happened in a person's life. It is a murderous deed, or any event in which human lives are sacrificed. To leave Jesus on the outside of your life is a tragedy.

A tragedy may be a frequent occurrence, or it may happen once in a great while. If a man goes down into a mine, lights a fuse of dynamite and fail to get out before it blows up, that is a tragedy. In the time of war when bombs are dropped on foreign soil and innocent men, women, and children are killed that is a tragedy.

When those oil tanks a few years ago blew up in Texas, and many lives were lost as a result of the explosion—that was a tragedy. When a man and his son's fishing boat overturns and they both are swept under the current and lost—that is a tragedy.

But, the greatest of all tragedies is that of <u>Leaving Jesus On The Outside Of your Life</u>.

In the language of the text.... *"Behold I stand at the door and knock, if any man will hear my voice and open the door, I will come in and sup with him, and he with me."*

This statement was first of all a message sent to a back-sliden church in Asia Minor. The best remedy for a back-sliden church is more communion with Christ.

This text belongs as much to the church of God as it does to the individual or the unconverted. We find Christ pictured as one being left on the outside of the church; having been driven away by her unkindness. But He does not go too far away. He loves the church too much to leave her altogether.... And he longs to return. He is well aware of the fact that the church will never prosper until He returns, so He just waits at the door post. He stands there waiting and knocking. I am saying today, that the greatest of all tragedies is that of <u>Leaving Jesus On The Outside Of Your Life</u>.

Christ knocks. He won't break the door open, and He won't come in unless He is invited. And, since the door is closed, there must be a definite act on our part or the door will never open and He will never enter. The conditions of entrance is so simple. All we need to do is just open the door. He says ... if any man, whether he be rich or poor, black or white, bond or free, regardless of his status or position in life ... *"If any man will hear my voice and open the door, I will come in and sup with him and he with me."*

I'm saying that the greatest tragedy is that of <u>Leaving Jesus On The Outside Of Your Life</u>.

I.   Christ Is Always On The Job

Christ is always on the job seeking entrance into the hearts of all of us. The heart seems to always be, by nature, closed against God. But thanks be to God, Christ is always on the job—anytime—morning, noon, or night; and He comes to us in so many different ways.

Sometimes He comes to us pouring out showers of blessing on our heads. Sometimes He picks us and makes us children of light. That is, blessings go all around everyone else and land on us. But we fail to see our blessings that are new every morning. Likened unto the animal under the acorn tree, we feast every day and fail to look up to see from whence cometh our supply.

Sometimes He comes to us in the form of sickness or afflictions, believing we may let Him in at that hour because we know that He is a physician that never lost a patient in all the world.

May I say here that it is a fine thing to hear His voice and open up the door of our heart and let Him in—for He is needed more on the inside than He is on the outside. It is a tragedy to leave Jesus on the outside.

II.   Sometimes He Is Left Outside Of The Family Life

You would be surprised at the number of children that have never heard their mother or their father pray. The reason you hear of confusion in churches is because there is always confusion in the home. Show me the one that keeps confusion going in the church, then follow them home and you will find the same thing.

It is the home that makes the churches, not the churches that make the home. Christ is needed on the inside of every home.

III.   Sometimes He Is Left On The Outside Of Churches

Although we sing praises to Him, we close our prayers in His name, but we believe it not. He is often left on the outside of our churches. You can just about tell when Christ is left on the outside of the church. How can we tell? We fail to love one another. We fail to treat our neighbor right. And then we lose the joy of our salvation.

I am wondering if you have heard of the painting of *Christ at the door*. I am told that when the painter turned the painting over to the critics for their appraisal or criticisms, they laughed at the painting; telling him that they were surprised that he had painted a man standing at an ordinary door but failing to put any type of a latch on the outside of that door. It is said that the artist sat down and wept because they failed to see the deeper meaning of his painting, and he said to them, "Gentlemen, the latch is on the inside."

I am saying today that the latch is on the inside. Many times Jesus remains on the outside for we fail to lift the latch and let Him in. It is a great tragedy to leave Jesus on the outside.

IV.   **Christ Is Often Left On The Outside Of Our Lives**

Where love is absent, Christ cannot be found. In the life of everyone, Christ should be on the inside. It is said that a man, in passing his neighbor's house, found him trying to scrape the frost off his window panes. He asked, "What are your doing there?" The neighbor's reply was, "I'm trying to get rid of this frost. I can't see out." The man then said to him, "There is a much easier way. Why not just light more fire on the inside."

I am led to believe that the reason we have so many people whose lives are cold and indifferent; so many people who fail to get a joy out of rendering service to the Lord; is only because we do not have enough fire kindled on the inside. If we let Christ in, He will be both guest and host. He says.… "*if anyone will hear my voice and open the door, I will come in and sup with him and he with me.*"

The greatest of all tragedies is that of leaving Jesus on the outside.

May I close with this thought—Tolstoy gives us a picture of a man in a boat which is pushed off from an unknown land. He is shown the opposite shore, given a pair of oars and left alone. He rows straight out into the stream. The current seizes the boat and swings it about.

All round him are other little boats, but the occupants of some have thrown their oars away. A few are bravely struggling with the current, but most are just gliding along and quite content. As one begins to row upstream against the current he cries, "Fool, I was to drift, but my oars prove to be my salvation".... And he escapes the destroying rapids and safely reaches the desired haven.

Less the meaning of the story be missed, the author put it down in black and white. He says the current represent the things of the world; the oars are our free will; and the opposite shore is God. The moral of this story is this—if we drift with the prevailing current of the world and fail to use the oars of our free will, the only goal which gives life its glory is lost.

The greatest tragedy is that of leaving Christ on the outside. Why not lift the latch and let Him in today.

SIX THINGS I KNOW GOD HAS DONE FOR ME
Scripture: Psalm 126:1-6

"The Lord has done great things for us; whereof we are glad."

Psalm 126:3

A minister was traveling through the country side to his church one day, and stopped to admire an abundant crop. He expressed his admiration to the farmer and then said, "You ought to thank God for blessing you with such a wonderful crop."

"What!"—said the farmer. "I do not see why I should thank God for it since it is all the result of the use of the proper fertilizers and my many hours of hard work."

The next year the minister visited the same farm, but he saw an entirely different picture. He found this same farmer complaining because his crop had failed. And, with a shepherd's heart of love he said—"One may work as hard and as long as he can; he may even make use of the proper fertilizers; but, if he lacks the blessings from God, it is impossible for him to succeed."

There are some things we can do for ourselves. There are some things that our relatives, friends and other people are able to do for us. But there are—Oh—so many things that we cannot do for ourselves and others cannot do them for us. If they are done for us, they are done only by the power of the Almighty God.

I am of the opinion that the highest sort of knowledge is to know God and to know yourself; and, if you would thoroughly know anything, you ought to teach it to others. Thus, my message this morning is more than just an ordinary sermon. It is my personal testimony. I've stopped by here on my way to heaven to tell you six things I know I didn't do for myself, and others didn't do for me; but <u>Six Things I Know God Has Done For Me</u>.

I.   **He Saved Me.**

In a meeting of the Salvation Army in London, England, one of the worse men of the city was converted. It was not long before some of his evil associates began to make fun of him. The conversation went like this—"You say you are a Christian ... so tell us something about Christ. Who was his father? Who was his mother? When did he live? How old was he when he died?"

To every question the man was asked he answered—"I just don't know."

Whereupon they said—"A fine Christian you are. You don't know a thing about Jesus Christ."

In reply the man looked in the faces of his critic and said—"I don't know much about Him it is true, but one thing I do know. I know He saved me."

This is one thing I know. I know He saved me. Like the Psalmist— He brought me up out of the marred clay; He set my feet on a rock and established my going; He has put a song in my heart.

God saved me—that's one thing I know God did for me.

II. **He Put Me In The Ministry.**

The other day a young man asked how did I happen to be a preacher. My reply was—"I didn't just happen to be a preacher. God made me a preacher when he put me in the ministry." It was one thing I couldn't and wouldn't do for myself; and I don't think I had anyone who hated me enough to do it for me. It was God.

I had many doubts and fears, but He put me in. I felt small, insignificant, and unworthy—but He put me in. There have been times when I have wanted out—but then there are times when I'm like Jeremiah—"*God's message is like fire shut up in my bones.*" I can't turn around and I can't quit, because God put me in the ministry.

III.   **He Has Given Me A Place, And A Place On His Program.**

I remember so well when I was being put though the test prior to my ordination. One aged minister said to me, after they had sweated me with a lot of difficult questions, "How would you feel toward this council if we saw fit not to pass on your ordination?"

My reply was—"Mister, I would love you just the same, and keep right on preaching the Gospel."

I have never worried about what man can do. Not boasting but, ever since I told the Lord I'd go, I've had somewhere to go. I'm a witness. He has opened doors for me; doors I wasn't able to see. I couldn't do it myself. Friends wouldn't, and couldn't do it for me. God has given me a place on His program.

IV.   **He Has Kept Me Alive.**

When I was a child I used to ride on the running board of my uncle's "Model T". One day I remember I decided to jump off while the automobile was moving. I didn't jump the way the car moved, but in the opposite direction. I was thrown head over heels in the ditch, and I laid unconscious for several hours. But—God kept me alive.

As a young man in the Marines, I caught it pretty tough. But—God kept me alive. And ever since I've been a soldier in His holy war, I've had my trials and tribulations; but He has been my rock in a weary land, my shelter in times of storm. He has kept me alive.

V.   **He Has Given Me A Heart To Love.**

A man tells of a terrible dream. He had done many evil things; he had cherished the wrong purposes in his heart; yet he was well thought of in the community. That night he had dreamed that he had made it to Heaven and he was walking the golden streets, wearing a long white robe. But to his surprise everyone kept staring at him and he felt uneasy and uncomfortable. Finally, he decided to look at himself. He discovered that his black heart shone through his white robe. When he awaken, he made up his mind that there was something in his heart he'd better change.

I don't know how it was with you, but I used to have a hard time keeping hatred out of my heart. If you hated me, I would hate in return. But God has given me the grace and power to bless them that curse me, and pray for them that despitefully use me. He has given me a heart to love.

VI. God Has Answered Many Of My Prayers.

God has not always answered my prayers as I have desired, but he has answered. He hasn't always given me what I have asked for, but since he knows what I need ever before I ask, I can truthfully say He has given me something. Sometimes it was better.

A man having only one leg and supporting himself on crutches made his way to church. A passerby watched and asked his companion, "Do you think the Lord will give that fellow another leg if he prays hard enough."

Over hearing the comment the cripple said to them—"I don't expect the Lord to give me another leg, but I do expect the Lord to answer my prayer to help me to make the best use of the one I have."

"The Lord has done great things for me—whereof, I am glad."

THE PROBLEM WITH PRESUMPTUOUSNESS
Scripture: Luke 14:8, 11

"When someone invites you to a wedding feast, do not take the place of honor, for a person more distinguished than you may have been invited. For everyone who exalts himself will be humbled, and he who humbles himself will be exalted."

All of us deep within us have what the late Dr. Martin Luther King, Jr. called the *"Drum Major Instinct"*.

We all want to be important, to assert ourselves, to achieve distinction, to lead the parade; the desire for recognition, this wish to be somebody, the yearning to be significant is our strongest emotion. And I think we will all agree that this drum major instinct is a basic and dominant impulse in human nature.

However, it is plainly taught in the sacred scriptures that we need to watch this dominant impulse of our nature, for it can get out of hand and it can be taken too far. We must be careful with this assertive drive, or it may become an arrogant presumptuous attitude that pushes and shoves and elbows other people out of the way.

To be presumptuous is to be arrogantly proud, overly bold, and to take undue liberties. Sometimes presumptuous people can be interpersonal in their relationships; they can be haughty, egotistical and unappreciative to the extent of taking other people for granted.

The presumptuous attitudes of people must have bothered Jesus greatly, because one of his most famous parables dealt with this secular human impulse of nature most of us have, and he suggested that presumptuous people are brought down by their own attitudes.

Apparently Jesus was invited to the home of a wealthy Pharisee. The dinner was attended by other prominent persons. He noticed with quiet amusement and with sad dismay, the scheming way the leaders worked to promote themselves. He noticed that there was an ugly unseeming rush to the tables, not so much for the food, but for the last seats, the place of prominence.

He noticed one self-appointed important person who made a mad rush for a seat of honor; but, when the host came in, he was embarrassed because the host called him down and another person up. Jesus said to his followers, "*Pay attention to what happened here. Avoid the sin of presumptuousness. When someone invites you to a wedding feast don't you take the place of honor, for a person more distinguished than you may also have been invited.*"

Jesus said in so many words—never be embarrassed by your own self important boldness.

Life is like this. Presumptuous people ultimately are called down. People who refuse to take the humble way are often humiliated. "*Everyone who exalts himself will be humbled, and he who humbles himself shall be exalted."*

On this Graduate's Day 1994, there are a few things I want to say especially to our graduated, but what I say to one, I must say to us all. A humble attitude beats the presumptuous attitude every time. The humble spirit is much better, much more Christ like than the arrogant, pushy presumptuous spirit. Before I go to my seat, there are some tricky presumptuous attitudes we need wary of as we walk on by faith each day.

I.   **Beware of presuming that you have all the answers.**

Beware of becoming arrogantly closed minded, thinking that "My way is the only way".

You must keep growing, stretching, learning. We must be humbly open to new truths from God.

How presumptuous it is to imagine that we have all the answers regarding God's magnificent and mysterious universe. Its like going down to the ocean believing that you can put the whole ocean in your pocket. God's universe is filled with mystery, and it is in the height of haughtiness to close the book on truth.

We are called to discipleship and a call to discipleship is to ever be a learner, to grow in the faith.

I recall a story of a little boy who fell out of the bed one night. His father rushed to check on him. He asked, "Son, pray tell me what happened?"

The boy said, "I really don't know but I guess I fell asleep too close to where I got in."

The same thing can happen to us. Presumptuously thinking we have all the answers. We can get the answers. We can get lazy and fall asleep too close to where we got in. We need to beware of presuming tat we have all the answers.

II. **Beware of presuming that you can be a winner on the front lines of today's battles without help.**

The scripture teaches us that there are some forces of evil in the world today. There are battles to be fought and victories to be won. Let no one tell you differently, the devil is the cause of it all.

He is a deceiver, a discourager, a divider, and a destroyer. His goal is to keep you from achieving your highest and best. He seeks to defame those who are worthy of appreciation and respect.

Each of us has an enemy that wants to destroy us. The only way we can be sure of factory over our enemy (the devil) is to stay as close to God as we can.

Beware of presuming that you can be a winner on the front line of today's battles without help. Having the Holy Spirit on the inside prepares you for any battle on the outside. Best to be plugged in to the power.

III. **Beware of presuming that God should bless you at the expense of others.**

I have read a number of religious magazines. Recently I came across an article by a business man entitled—<u>How God Answered My Prayer</u>. This businessman and a co-worker were being considered for the same prestigious position with their company. The man said he really wanted the job so he prayed about it; and just before the selection was made, the co-worker had a heart attack and was hospitalized, which meant he was taken out of consideration. He got the Job. He concluded "That's how I got the job".

How presumptuous to think that God, our Heavenly Father, would give one of His children a heart attack to promote and answer the prayer of another child. Never be that presumptuous.

We must be careful in our prayer that we are not presumptuous; that we don't ask God to bless us at the expense of others.

God has the same rules. and standards, and requirements for success for each and everyone alike. Someone has said, the elevator to success is never working—each one has to take the stairs.

Beware of presuming that God should bless us at the expense of others.

IV. **Beware of presuming that our wants are more important than God's will.**

Some times what we want and what God wants is the same thing. But, oftimes they are not, and we need to be open to that. To follow in the footsteps of the Master, we have to recall that there in the garden of Gethsemane He had problems of going to the Cross. He said, *"Father, if at all possible let this cup pass from me."* But He didn't stop there. He went on to say, *"Not my will but thine be done."*

Thy will be done in that testing scene of His life, we see the perfect picture of humble religion—the opposite of presumptuous religion.

One writer has said—"Not for one single day can I discern my way. But this I surely know. He who gives the day will show the way, so I securely go."

Belief in God's word, plus surrender to God's will, equals trust in God's goodness.

CHAPTER II

"But seek ye first the Kingdom of God, and His righteousness; and all these things shall be added unto you."

Matthew 6:33

George was a few hours from finishing Tennessee State University, when Dr. Ralph W. Riley, President of the American Baptist Theological Seminary, shared with him a letter Dr. Riley had received from Reverend James H. Dotson, the Pastor of Mt. Zion Baptist Church in Tulsa, Oklahoma. Rev. Dotson's letter stated that he was looking for a young man who would be able to work throughout the church as well as assist in the preaching ministry. George started immediate correspondences with Rev. Dotson.

> *"All of my preaching experience had been standing in for pastors who were on vacation, ill, or had other speaking engagements. The President of my seminary knew this and asked me if I was interested in coming to Tulsa."*

On the second Sunday in August 1953, young George Calvin McCutchen graduated with honors from Tennessee State University in Nashville with a Bachelor of Science degree, and arrived in Tulsa on Wednesday of that same week to meet and talk with Reverend Dotson.

> *"I arrived by train at 6:00 a.m. No one met me. I took a cab to Mt. Zion's parsonage, 417 North Elgin, and met Mrs. Dotson on the porch. She gave the cab driver a note to take me to 761 North Greenwood, the home of Mrs. Francis Franklin, where a room had been reserved for me. I met Pastor Dotson about 1:00 p.m. that*

day. We had a lengthy visit, and he showed me the church building about 4:00 p.m."

George Calvin McCutchen preached his first sermon at Mt. Zion on the Third Sunday in August 1953 at the 11:00 a.m. service. His subject, based on the familiar story of the prodigal son, was—"A Made Up Mind Put Into Action".

The pastor, his family, the officers and members of Mt. Zion received this young man warmly. Because of Pastor Dotson's failing health, young McCutchen was made the Assistant Pastor, and given the task of preaching for all the worship services and funerals. For this position as Assistant Pastor, he was paid a weekly salary of forty dollars ($40.00) plus room and board. He stayed at the home of Mrs. Francis Franklin, a Deaconess of the church. Mrs. Franklin was paid $12.50 per week for his room and board. For this she washed his clothes, prepared two meals a day (breakfast and dinner) and took his phone calls.

The attendance each Sunday morning and evening increased. He attended all board and auxiliary meetings and visited the sick and shut-ins. He brought hope and inspiration to the congregation that had been through many struggles and challenges since the *"1921 Race Riot".*

One year after George Calvin McCutchen came to Tulsa in 1953, there was one young lady attending a 6:00 a.m. prayer meeting at the church that grasped his attention and caught his heart. That was Miss Adelene Deborah Dixon, a registered nurse who was working at Morton Hospital. After several months of courting, George and Adelene were married August 23, 1954 at her father's home in Hammond, Louisiana.

Mrs. Franklin invited the young couple to stay in her home. Mrs. Franklin really didn't like being alone, and for a few weeks she cooked for the both of them. When they decided to get a place of their own, the McCutchen's moved to the Thompson's Apartments at 1712 N. Rockford. Of course, the move to their own apartment meant furniture had to be purchased and rent had to be paid; therefore, Mt. Zion added to the $40.00 per week salary the $12.50 which they had been giving Mrs. Franklin. Adelene continued her nursing career and George continued as Assistant Pastor of Mt. Zion.

After three years of marriage, Adelene and George McCutchen were expecting their first child. Adelene's plans were to work until the child was born, then stay home at least two or three years with the child before returning to work. The family budget included both salaries and it was next to impossible for the family to survive only with the salary George was receiving from Mt. Zion. It was discussed by the Trustees to increase the Assistant's salary, but they could not see where they would get these extra funds. Pastor Dotson had allowed his salary to be decreased to help the church, but with the agreement that it would not be used to increase the salary of anyone else.

In the meanwhile, the Reverend J. Castina Jackson, Director of The Baptist Educational Center, was hired to be the Co-Pastor at Paradise Baptist Church because of the illness of Reverend. H. L. Branch. His position with the Southern Baptist was now open, and George McCutchen was approached about becoming his successor. The requirements were Seminary and College training and at least a year's Pastoral experience.

Young George was well liked by the Pastors of the North Tulsa community. He was offered the position and hired to become the Director of the North Tulsa Baptist Center.

NOTE: This sermon has taken on several names with the passing years, but it was the first sermon prepared and preached by Dr. McCutchen at Mt. Zion on the 3rd Sunday in August 1953. It was originally entitled "A Made Up Mind Put Into Action".

THE GOOD EXAMPLE OF A BAD MAN
Scripture: Luke 15:18-24

"I will arise and go to my father, and will say unto him, father, I have sinned against heaven and before thee.

Luke 15:18

Not without reason, this has been called the greatest short story in the world.

Under the Jewish law, a father was not free to leave his property as he liked. The elder son must get two thirds and the younger one third. It was by no means unusual for a father to distribute his estate before he died. Therefore, the younger son came to his father one day and said—"Father I want you to give me the part of the estate I will get anyway when you are dead, and let me get out of here and on my own."

The father didn't argue. He knew that if the son was ever to learn, he must learn the hard way and he granted his request.

Without delay the son realized his share of the property and left home. He soon ran through the money, and ended up feeding pigs—a task that was forbidden to a Jew.

As long as a man is away from God, he is not truly himself. Thus Jesus paid sinning mankind the greatest compliment it has ever been paid "when he came to himself".

He was only truly himself when he decided to go back to God and to home.

He decided to go back home, not as a son, nor as a slave, but as a hired servant.

The hired servants were lower in rank than a slave. They were only day laborers. The ordinary slave, in a sense, was a member of the family; but a hired servant could be dismissed at a day's notice. He was not one of the family at all.

He came home and the record shows the father never gave him the chance to ask to be a servant. Instead the father ordered his servants to bring the son a robe for his body, a ring for his finger and shoes for his bare feet. The robe stood for honor, the ring for authority, and the shoes meant he was taken back as a member of the family; for the children of the family were shod, whereas slaves were not. A feast was also made that all might rejoice at the wanderer's return.

Let's stop there and see the truth thus far in this parable. I take the position—this should never have been referred to as the "Parable of the Prodigal Son" for the son is not the hero of the story. It should have been called the "Parable of the Loving Father", for it tells us more about the father's love than it tells of the son's sins.

Now, I used to look upon this young man as being a disgrace to the human race. But, regardless to how bad one is, there is always some good in them, if you look long enough and try hard enough to find it. Therefore, I thought to point out some of the good qualities as seen in this life.

So now, I'm asking you to pull up a chair and listen as I talk about "The Good Example Of A Bad Young Man".

I. **He Asked For His Part.**

Everyone in the family has a part. He wanted what belonged to him. He asked only for his share of the property.

II. **He Took A Journey Into A Far Country.**

He was desirous of sowing some *wild oats*, so he decided to go into a far country rather than staying around home and bringing disgrace upon his family.

III. **He Went To Work.**

After he had spent all and began to be in want, he got himself a job and went to work. He joined himself not with the pimps and racketeers, but a citizen.

IV. **He Did Not Stay Down.**

He found himself in a pig's pen, but he didn't stay there. The only way people drown in deep water is not by falling in, but it is by staying there.

V. **He Came To His Senses.**

He came to his senses before it was too late. Some folk are fools all their lives. Some folk never get over *fool's hill*. He talked to himself.

Folk ought to talk to themselves. What are you saying to yourself? The Bible says the wages of sin is death. Quit before pay day.

VI. **He Made Up His Mind.**

He made up his mind then he put his mind into action. He was willing to go home on his father's terms. It was not faith, hope, love—not even prayer, but it was time that brought him home.

A ROCK TO STAND ON FOREVER
Scripture: Matthew 16:13-18

God has blessed you Simon, son of Jonah, Jesus said. For my Father in Heaven has personally revealed this to you. This is not from any human source. You are Peter—a stone, and upon this rock I will build my church. And all the powers of hell shall not prevail against it."

Matthew 16:17-18

The Empire State Building in New York City stands 103 stories tall. It is 1,253 feet in height, which is a quarter of a mile high; and this building contains ten million bricks, six thousand windows, 75 miles of water pipes, 5,000 telephones, and two million feet of electric wiring. This huge structure, which weighs in the excess of 303,000 tons, needed a tremendous foundation. It is reported that the architects and engineers excavated down beneath the earth until they reached solid granite (which is the basic rock of the earth) and upon this rock the Empire State Building was built.

This famous building has stood, and will stand, for centuries because it is built on a solid rock rather than on the shifting sand. Every building must have a solid, firm foundation if it is to be able to stand. As it is with huge buildings, so it is with our lives. In times like these and in a world like ours, we need something solid, secure, and rock-like to stand on. This world in which we live is characterized by trembling, shaking, swinging, tottering, and agitating, and I say we need something solid, secure, and rock-like on which to stand.

There are many kinds of rocks. Thousands of young people enjoy collecting rocks as a hobby. There are common rocks, metamorphic rocks, and sedimentary rocks; rocks of all kinds and colors. But, this world needs most of all, not a rock to collect, not a "pet" rock, but a rock to survive and a rock on which to stand.

I need not tell you that men, women, boys, and girls are having and experiencing hard and difficult times. Standing tall, standing strong, standing sure, standing long, and even standing at all are great achievements and great attainments in times like these and in this our day. The prime and primary need of this world and this world's people is finding, getting, and securing a rock to stand on forever.

The Bible submits just such a rock that is needed in these times, and in times like these. Let me put your minds at ease for fear someone might tune me out before I have finished this message—JESUS CHRIST is the rock on which you can stand forever.

I shall give you the sad part of the message first, which is this—in spite of all Jesus has done, is doing, and will do, man is still trying to find another rock upon which to stand.

I.   **The Rock of Materialism**

Many people have turned to the rock of materialism. Some people are of the philosophical opinion that the gathering of material goods and worldly possessions constitutes the greatest good and the highest value in life. Because some can pride themselves in the ownership of a home in a good neighborhood; because they can boast of two cars in the garage; because some can talk of their many suits and dresses with matching shoes, in their walk-in closets; and because they can boast of their countless dollars in the bank, they get the idea that they have it made.

This is seen in the fact that they seem to turn their noses up at the less fortunate. They snobbishly seem to have the idea that when God made them, he got out of the people making business and left them the only pebble on the beach. There is, of curse, something wrong with this rock as a sure place to stand. Life is fluctuating, fleeting, and changing. It is entirely possible for one to have a lot of the world's good today and have nothing tomorrow.

Ask the Prodigal Son about the "hog pens" of this world and he will tell you that there is a "hog pen" for every person who builds his life on what he has in his pocket or on his person.

Jesus asked the question one day— *"For what shall it profit a man if he should gain the entire world and loose his own soul?"*

Money, material things, even gold or silver, will ultimately pass away. Thus, we need a rock of a more lasting quality on which to stand.

II. The Rock of Intellectualism

There are those who are determined to stand on the rock of intellectualism. These are the people who estimate their success by the many schools they have attended and the number of degrees and certificates of higher learning they have received. Education is a wonderful thing in this world. You cannot get far without it. But, education must include knowledge of what to do with it. One is better off to get an education and then get over it. A college education never hurt anyone who was willing to learn something afterward. But, remember this—a child educated only at school, is an uneducated child.

I would submit to you right here that it is entirely possible for a man or a woman, youth and/or adult, to be sure enough to have their heads together in terms of degrees but, if their heart is not right, they are still on a drifting sand foundation. Head and heart must be together with—God calling the shots, or you have no firm and lasting foundation on which to stand.

III. The Rock of Moral Goodness

Then there are those who would stand on the rock of moral goodness. These are they who boast of merely living by the golden rule, and they that brag about being just as good as those who go to church and follow Jesus. But, I don't care how good you are, or how good you think you are, you are not good enough to save yourself. The Bible says—*"For all have sinned and come short of the glory of God."* (Romans 3:23); *"All we like sheep have gone astray ... "* (Isaiah 53:6); *"All our unrighteousness are as filthy rags in His sight."* (Isaiah 54:5).

The rock of moral goodness is not solid enough. The good news is that God meets us where we are because we cannot rise to where he want us to be.

And this brings us to the last part of this message.

IV. **Searching For Rocks To Stand On Forever**

There are many in this world today that are still searching for rocks to stand on forever. I submit to you that there is but one, and only one, who is safe, secure, and steadfast; and, that one is JESUS CHRIST, our Lord. Jesus Christ is the rock that we can stand on forever.

Some rocks deteriorate and degenerate over and through the years. The tough and rough winds of time, fire, and flood beat upon their brow and eat away at their ability and capacity. But Jesus is the same yesterday, today, and forever.

Jesus is a sure rock in a weary land and a shelter in the times of a storm. Jesus is a sure **Rock of Companionship**. "*He is a friend that sticks closer than a brother*" (Proverbs 28:22). "*When my father and my mother forsake me, then the Lord will take me up*" (Psalm 27:10).

Jesus is a **Solid Rock of Directorship**. "*Trust in the Lord with all thine heart, and lean not to thine own understanding; in all thy ways acknowledge Him and He shall direct thy paths*" (Proverbs 3:5-6).

And, most of all, Jesus Christ is the **Solid Rock of Saviorship**. John writes—"*For God so loved the world ...* " (John 3:16); Paul wrote—"*For ye know the grace of our Lord, Jesus Christ, that though He was rich, for your sakes he became poor that we through His poverty might be rich.* " (II Corinthians 8:9).

I don't know about you, but I'm going to stand on a rock that will stand forever. When my way is dark and dreary—I'm going to stand on the rock that will stand forever. You may see me struggling and striving, but don't worry about me—I am standing on a rock that will stand forever. You may see me crying and shedding briny tears, but don't worry about me—I'm standing on a rock that will stand forever. You may see me rising, falling, stumbling, and bumbling; don't worry about me—I'm standing on a rock that will stand forever.

One day I may be weighed down with sickness, sorrow, adversity, and affliction. One day I will climb my last hill of difficulty, jump my last ditch of sorrow, and will have to walk into the valley and the shadow of death; but, don't worry about me—I will still be standing on a rock that will stand forever.

ARE YOU STILL CARRYING YOUR WATERPOT
Scripture: John 4:28-29

"The woman then left her water pot, and went her way into the city and saith to men: Come see a man which told me all things that I did."

John 4:28-29

The story of Jesus and this woman at the well is one of the most well known and beloved passages of scripture in the Bible. It's a story which retains its freshness and excitement every time it is told and heard. It contains some of the most profound lessons to be found in sacred scripture. It also let us know that some of the problems of society which are prevalent today were in existence when Christ walked among us while He was here on earth.

We learn from this scripture that racial hatred is no new thing. It was as severe over 1900 years ago as it was during the 60's here, and as it is in South Africa now. We also learn that immoral practices and loose living was just as common while Jesus was on earth, as it is today. We also learn that those persons who have the most skeletons in their closets are the ones generally who have the most hang ups concerning their religious practices.

We have before us today this woman of Samaria who had led a lifestyle which could have been filmed into a rated triple X movie, yet she is found arguing with Jesus concerning the proper place to worship God. Today, however, we want to look at this woman in a different light.

The fact that she left her water pot at the well is very significant. You see, this water pot was a symbol of her past. It represented all the sinful acts and unrighteous deeds she had ever done. It shows us that after a brief meeting with Jesus she left her water pot behind and became an instant missionary.

A careful look at this woman, her ways and her actions after she met the Lord, prompted me, with the aid of the Divine Spirit, to talk today from this all important subject which is a question—<u>Are You Still Carrying Your Water Pot?</u>

I. **Observe first—Leaving Water Pots Is Not easy, But Not Impossible.**

This woman of Samaria, we commonly call the woman at the well, had at least three hang ups. All of her hang ups were carried around in her water pot. She had a hang up on race, she had a hang up on morals, and she had a hang up on worship.

She was opinionated. She had, yes, some strange convictions and, although she had no way of substantiating any of her beliefs, she was set in her ways and didn't mind defending her position. Her hang up on race brought her all the way from Sychar to Jacob's well at noonday. Jesus asked her for a drink of water and she proceeded to give him her entire outlook on life.

"You are a Jew," she said, "I am a Samaritan. The way you Jews feel about us—you got to be kidding." A racial hang up was in the water pot.

The conversation continued until Jesus had pointed to her hang up on morals. *"Go!"* Jesus said—*"Go fetch your husband, bring him back with you. I have blessings for your entire house."*

His words hit her with a sudden shock and she suddenly caught sight of herself. Jesus knew she didn't have a husband, but wanted her to admit it. When she said "I don't have one", it gave Jesus the opportunity to tell her some things about herself that she thought nobody knew but herself.

Jesus said in so many words—your bedroom has been but a temporary stopping place for five men and the one you have now, you haven't had the decency to go to the court house and make it legal. But now you have hit rock bottom. You have picked up another woman's drop-out, allowed him to hang his coat in your closet, put his feet under your table, and sleep in your bed. You can't tie the knot because you haven't untied the last knots. You are presently making a fool out of yourself just to have a man around the house.

She had a hang up on morals—this she was carrying around in her water pot.

She also had a hang up on worship. When Jesus told her about her past life, He upset her and she proceeded to change the subject. She said, "You some kind of a preacher or a prophet—let's talk about worship."

She was more concerned about place than she was about motive. She was more concerned about where and when, than she was about how. This hang up, she was carrying around in her water pot.

To end the conversation she said to him—"Well, we are expecting a Savior and a redeemer, and I guess I'll just keep on doing what I'm doing until he comes."

Jesus said, "Let me introduce myself. I am your redeemer. I am your Savior and Lord."

The Bible says this woman *"left her water pot and went her way into the city, and saith to men—come see a man which told me all things I ever did."*

Leaving water pots is not easy, but not impossible.

The second thought is this:

II. **New Life In Christ Causes One To Leave Water Pots Behind.**

While Jesus was talking, something began to happen to her. She opened up her heart and the *living water* started flowing in, and all of her hang ups started flowing out. She opened her heart and God's grace flowed in and the impurities of her life flowed out. She got a new outlook on life; her thoughts were new; she got a new walk and a new talk. Somebody said—her water pot went one way and she went another.

She became an instant missionary. She went uptown saying come see—not a Black man or White Man, not a Jewish man, or even a Samaritan man—but a God sent man who told me everything that I did. I met him and I want you to meet him too.

He looked beyond my faults and He saw my needs. He looked beyond denomination and gave me regeneration. He looked beyond my reputation and gave me salvation. He, the man down there at the well, looked beyond all my hang ups and gave me a chance to straighten up.

New life in Christ causes one to leave water pots behind. Permit me to ask one more time—<u>Are You Still carrying Your Water Pot</u>?

The final thought is:

III. **When One's Thirst has been quenched with the water of life, water pots are unnecessary.**

Leaving the water pot behind was a part of the testimony of a changed woman. She came to Jesus with at least three hang ups—carrying them around with her water pot; but the record shows that she didn't leave as she came carrying her water pot.

Jesus met this woman at the point of her greatest need. Jesus saw more than her sins. He saw more than she really was. He looked beyond her faults and saw her needs. He discerned her thirst for the water of life. He was not interested in winning an argument; He was interested in winning her.

Once her thirst was quenched with the water of life, her water pot was unnecessary. She became a transformed enthusiast.

Just as the Disciples left their boats and nets, and Matthew left his receipt of custom to follow Jesus, she left her old life style, old ways, and old loyalties. She left her water pot to follow Jesus.

All too often we come in contact with people who say they have met the Lord; they've been born again; they've been washed in the blood of the Lamb, but they are still carrying their old water pots. They have water pots of selfishness, pride, envy, jealousy, gossip, and hate.

I think I need to tell us if you really know Christ for yourself, you will live your water pots behind.

THE WISDOM OF SELF-EXAMINATION
Scripture: Matthew 7:1-5

*"And why beholdest thou the mote that is in thy brother's eye,
but considerest not the beam that is in thine own eye."*

Mathew 7:3

It is the common practice of men to single out and magnify the faults of his brother—terming them as being large and evident, while thinking of his own faults as being small and insignificant. But there is wisdom in self-examination.

I am told that every merchant closes up shop at least once a year for the purpose of taking an inventory. This inventory shows him just where he stands. It not only reveals to him his failures and weaknesses in the past, but it also serves as a guide for future operations.

Likewise, each person who is in earnest about his religion must stop often and take inventory, in order to see how he stands; to determine his failures and weaknesses in the past so that he might redeem himself in the future. For there is wisdom in self-examination.

Now this mote that Jesus speaks about is those small particles that are seen in rays of sunshine. The beam is a large piece of timber, a joist, a rafter. The mote is a graphic representation of a comparatively little fault, while the beam is the symbol of large faults. And Jesus, desiring His disciples to be true to themselves asked—*"Why beholdest thou the mote that is in thy brother's eye and considerest not the beam that is in thine own eye"*.

What is He saying?

I.   **Man Must Seek The Better Understanding of Himself.**

He is saying first of all that man must seek the better understanding of himself.

Let us observe our attitude toward our brother. We are prone to check on him so closely that we can discern a little mote, a little speck of dust in his eye; but we can look all around that beam that is in our own, and pull out the smallest fault of our neighbor.

The reason for that is this—that great and glorious opinion of ourselves blinds us to our own faults and turns our attention to the faults of our brother. We look at our neighbor's errors with a microscope, and look at ours through the wrong end of the telescope.

We have two sets of weights and measures—one for home use and one for foreign. Every vice has two names—a name to flatter or minimize if it is our own, but a name to play it up or enlarge if it belongs to a neighbor.

We strain gnats and swallow camels, we wash the outside of the platter clean, but on the inside we leave filled with dead men's bones. We seek the cleanliness of our neighbor's house while ours is left dirty.

And who can truthfully say—I am better than my neighbor? *"Why beholdest thou the mote that is in thy brother's eye and considerest not the beam that is in thine own".*

Yes, Jesus would have us seeking the better understanding of ourselves.

II.   **Man Must be Careful Not to Condemn Others.**

Not only must man seek the better understanding of himself, but he must be careful not to condemn in others the same thing he is allowing to exist in himself.

Listen as He speaks further … *"How can you say to your brother let me pull the mote out of thine eye, when lo and behold there is a beam in thine own eye?"*

This thing might be done, but let me say first of all that it is dangerous. There is a danger that comes from man and a greater danger that comes from God. In the eyes of men, the critic becomes very unpopular. Jesus didn't like hypocrisy and neither do men. The danger that comes from God is this—He told us that He will deal with us in the same manner that we deal with our neighbor. If we do not forgive them, God will not forgive us. As long as we make it our business to point out the sins of others, there is no hope that our sins will be blotted out.

To work on your neighbor when you are not right yourself is futile. While there is a beam in your own eye, it is impossible to move the mote from your brother's eye. To do so is to perform a very delicate operation. Any impaired vision will result in an awkward attempt that will cause much pain, and yet will not affect its purpose.

No, the beam has to go first. While a man is blinded to his own sin, he cannot save his neighbor. A Christian must seek deliverance from his own sins before he can work on the sins of his brother.

The physician must first heal himself. The prophet can't afford to be a bigger sinner than the people he is denouncing, and that is why Jesus says—*"Thou hypocrite, cast the beam out of thine own eye, then thou canst see clearly to cast the mote out of thy brother's eye."*

He was saying that it is a bad thing to be condemning in others that what we are allowing to exist in ourselves.

III. **Take Time Out For a Spiritual Checkup.**

Note next, every Christian should take some time out for a spiritual checkup. He should concern himself about the following questions.

Who am I?—Do I look to myself first?

- Am I unduly proud of myself?
- Am I indifferent to the welfare of other?
- Am I over confident in my judgment of other?
- Am I selfish?
- Am I a lover of honors and praises?
- Who am I?
- Who am I to God?
- What is God to me?

We need to sweep the dirt away from our own doorsteps before we attempt to sweep our neighbor's

One writer has said, "If we love ourselves so much, how can we love God enough?"

If we are so busy serving ourselves, how can we serve God? Yes, every Christian should have a spiritual checkup. He should ask himself the question—have I given anything today; have I helped

some needy soul on his way; from the dawn till setting sun, have I
wounded anyone; shall I reap for what I have done today.

IV.   Yes, There Is Wisdom In Self-Examination.

If we are through and honest with ourselves, we get four results
from self-examination. Self-examination first of all will bring true
and sincere humility. Self-examination makes us humble. When we
face up to our own sins, we cannot fail to be sorry and to realize
that we are very weak children of the most high God; and we say
in deep humility that we have no power within ourselves to help
ourselves. We will then turn to God to forgive us and to cleanse us
both outwardly in our bodies, and inwardly in our hearts.

Then self-examination leads to a greater surge of thankfulness.
Our God is so forgiving and kind. When we have failed, He always
gives us strength and courage to try again.

Self-examination also makes us more tolerant of others. When we
see how weak and full of faults we are, we have more understanding,
and we are more patient with others.

And fourth, self-examination should bring determination. When
we find out just how bad we are doing, their should be something
within us that would make us cry out—with the help of the Lord I
am going to do better. Yes, there is wisdom in self-examination.

V.   Keep Looking Up

Note last, but not least, that a Christian is supposed to keep
looking up. He is to keep looking toward the sky rather than the
muck and the mire. There is no future in looking forever to the dark
side of things. Why go around with your head bowed. Why feel that
life is dark and gloomy. Keep looking up.

We close by telling this story.

A young man was walking along the street one day when he happened
to see on the ground before him a two dollar bill. Someone had lost it
and it was his good luck to find it, but it turned out to be his bad luck
in the end. From that very day on, this boy kept his eyes turned toward
the ground hoping to find another two dollar bill or something else of
value.

Twenty-five years passed and the man had collected a cigar box of pins, buttons, a number of small coins, and a variety of things that had fallen by the wayside. Perhaps those things were worth picking up, but not when you consider what happened to the man himself.

From stooping over so much, the man became a hunch back and developed trouble with his lungs. And worse than that, this poor fellow— looking for the little values, missed the things of greater value in life. He missed the smiles of his neighbors and the beauty of the world about him; the sky, the landscapes, and the flowers.

Always looking downward toward the pavement, the poor fellow developed a bad habit of looking down in other ways. He became a grouch, a pessimist, and an "old meany". His relatives had little respect for him; his neighbors shunned him; little children were afraid of him; and he couldn't hold a job anywhere he went. His health became poor, and he went to his grave a miserable and wretched man.

How much better would it have been for him to have gone through life with his chin up looking at the sky or into the friendly eyes of people as they passed by. These values would have enriched his life more than two dollar bills, pins, and buttons.

A Christian should go through life looking up, lifting others, laughing, and loving. For what ever you have in your heart, whether it be love or hatred, it is contagious. It will run from heart to heart, and from breast to breast. I don't know about you but, I'm going to press on until Jesus calls me home.

THE SON THAT STAYED HOME
Scripture: Luke 14: 11-32

'And he answering said to this father, Lo these many years have I served thee, neither transgressed I at any time thy commandments; and yet thou never gave me a kid that I might make merry with my friends."

Luke 15:29

Some time ago I talked to you about the return of the prodigal son. In that message I spoke concerning him from the young man's point of view. In that, I didn't play up the bad in him, but rather called upon the New Testament to prove that he wasn't so bad after all.

I believe I said that it wasn't any harm in asking for his part, and that's what he did. And then he took a journey into a far country, not wishing to bring shame and disgrace on his family. Spending all that he had, he didn't start robbing and stealing, but rather got himself a job and went to work, accepting a lowly task—being sent into the fields to feed the swine.

And there in that condition, thinking of his father's house, where the hired servants had bread and enough to spare, he makes up his mind and comes on back home. Not on his own terms, but on his father's terms. In a penitent spirit he said, "I am not worthy to be called thy son. Just make me one of the hired servants."

He came on back home. The father seeing him coming, runs out to meet him, falls on his neck and kisses him saying—bring the best robe and place it on him; get shoes for his feet; get a ring and place in on his finger; and he orders the servants to go and kill the fatted calf, for his son was lost but now found, was blind but now sees. And he throws a great feast, gathering in all the friends, and they began to make merry because of the son's return.

They were proving the Master's point that there is more rejoicing in Heaven over one sinner that repents, than ninety and nine "just" persons who need no repentance.

But, there is a brother. The elder brother he was; who, when returning from the field hears the music and all the merry making, and inquires as to the meaning of all this. The servants tell him, "Why, don't you know your brother came back home today, and your father is so happy that he has killed that fatted calf, and we are having a celebration."

Upon hearing this news, he doesn't rejoice as the others, but rather becomes disgusted. So much so that he decided he would tell his father just what he thought about the whole thing. And he says, "*Father, I have served you lo these many years, and not once have I transgressed any of your commandments, and yet you never gave me a kid that I may make merry with my friends. I just can't understand it. But as soon as this, thy son who ran away from you, wasted his goods on the harlots, and came running back here empty handed, you have killed for him the fatted calf."*

This is an ugly text. It is a cross between a snarl and a whine, yet it is the testimony of a very earnest and upright man; one who had spent all of his life in his father's house. According to his own testimony, he had been the most dutiful son. As a matter of fact, he had been perfect—yet all his uprightness and industry had brought him nothing. He places a charge on his father that he really couldn't deny.

Of course it was the elder son's fault that he had nothing. The father was eager to share his very all with him, and this was his reply to the son—*"You have always been with me and all I have is thine ... "*

But in spite of his father's eagerness, he was as much disgusted as the other son who found himself in a far country.

There is something about this elder son, this brother that stayed at home, that we really don't admire at all. Perhaps, it is his attitude. There is something in a person's attitude that either lowers or elevates a person in one's estimation of them. I have seen people hired on a job; good workers they were; but they would stay there a while and then come up missing. You go to the supervisor and ask—*where's Joe,* the reply may be—he was fired today. You may ask—*on what grounds was he fired, he was a good worker;* and be told—yes, but no one liked his attitude.

So I have come to the conclusion that a person's attitude can make all the difference in the world. But, what can we say bout this elder brother? What of his attitude? Were his actions justifiable?

I am sure if we were in search for the abundant life, we wouldn't think of asking him were to find it. Even Jesus, with his keen eye for the best in us, didn't relate that there was any good in this brother. So we must examine the scriptures carefully and see first if we can bring out the good in him.

Always look for the best in a person. If you can't find it in him and the story does not bring it out, call him up and let him speak for himself. So, what can we say in his favor.

I.   **He Was An Honest And Upright Man**

Since he represents the typical Pharisee, you can rest assured that he was an honest and upright man. He was utterly free from the ugly sin of the flesh. He had been found in the fields, in a clean environment. He was in a clean environment because of his own choice. He was there because he wanted to be there.

But where was his brother? He was in a pig's pin; in a foul and filthy environment. And, he wasn't there because he really wanted to be there; but because of the sin of flesh, the waste of his funds, and his adverse circumstance put him there. Yes, this elder brother was clean, the other was not. By that we say that he was leagues ahead of his brother. But, was he?

II. **He Was A Worker**

The fact that he was in the field indicates that he was a worker, and work is every man's obligation.

Bernard Shaw says that "a gentleman is one who puts into life more than he takes out of it". According to that, he was on his way to being a gentleman. Work is the way to self respect. Even my Master worked, for He said— *"I must work the works of Him who sent me while it is yet day, for the night cometh."*

But while he was working, his brother was wasting. So, in this case he was leagues ahead of his brother and did not realize it.

III. **He Was Making A contribution**

Being a clean and earnest worker, he was making a contribution. As far as this prodigal was concerned, the farm could be turned back into the wilderness or the whole place could topple over into ruins. But the elder brother kept the farm going. He kept the place capable of receiving his brother when his good times were all over.

So, in three instances he was leagues ahead and stood shoulders higher than his brother. But, in spite of it all, he is very disappointing to us. What is the matter with him? Why is he so disappointing?

He had one central defect. Though he was a member of the same family, he was totally lacking the family spirit of loyalty and goodwill. He found himself on good terms with neither his brother not his father. Though he was bound up in a family of others, he still insisted on acting as though he was a *lone wolf.*

Had he been interested enough, he probably could have prevented his brother from leaving home. He might have talked him out of it. It seems that he was declaring that it was none of his business; holding that he was broad-minded and he believed in letting everyone go to torment in their own way.

There is no sin more dangerous than that of indifference. Many of us fall into this category. We have the ability to look upon the woes and wounds of others and be totally unmoved by them. He failed to be concerned about his brother going away, and had no joy in his return.

The father was glad beyond words. The home atmosphere was vibrant with happiness. Even the hired servants took part in the rejoicing—but not this elder brother. Some said that he had a righteous anger, if there is such a thing. I don't think he had that; because, if there is such a thing, it is born of love instead of selfishness and hate, and it seeks to help and not to hurt.

What are we saying? Try to be a part of the fellowship. Rejoice with those who rejoice, weep with those who weep, and praise God for full salvation.

CHAPTER III

"For my God shall supply all your needs according to His riches in glory by Christ Jesus."

Philippians 4:19

There was much prayerful consideration given to this offer. Leaving Mt. Zion was not an easy decision to make. He must give up the chance of becoming the pastor of Mt. Zion; his wife was pregnant with their first child; she would soon go on maternity leave from her nursing position at Morton; there was no promise or prospect of a raise in his $52.50 weekly salary. Two things helped George McCutchen make this decision—

> *"First, I hadn't asked the Lord who put me into the ministry to make me a Pastor. My only goal was to hold a job that was religious in nature. Secondly, the salary increase came as an answered prayer."*

January 1956 George Calvin McCutchen assumed the duties as the new Director of the North Tulsa Baptist Educational Center. He gave Mt. Zion a ninety day notice, and worked both jobs for that period.

This new job gave him the opportunity to work with and for all the pastors of North Tulsa. Dr. T. Oscar Chappelle, Sr. was his supervisor; board members were Dr. Calvin K. Stalnaker, Rev. Theodore Rowland, Rev. C. L West, and Rev. H. D. Morris. His salary tripled what he was receiving and, with both salaries, Adelene gave up her work at the hospital.

Rev. McCutchen enjoyed the work as a Teacher-Missionary in Tulsa. He preached somewhere almost every Sunday; kept his tithes paid at Mt. Zion; but was only asked to return to Mt. Zion to preach a couple of funerals where the family and Pastor asked him to preach; and one fifth

Sunday, the young adults requested that he deliver the Sunday Morning message.

> *"I recall preaching one Sunday morning at the Pilgrim Rest Baptist Church on Norfork for Rev. L. V. Price. The church was under construction, and the building had a dirt floor. It was a rainy Sunday morning and water had been running into the building. I stepped into the water, then into the mud and dirt. It collected on m shoes and my feet were almost too heavy to move around in the pulpit."*

After George's 90 days had expired, Pastor Dotson secured the service of Reverend Alton Bryant; a little later, the Reverend R. D. Drew. Pastor Dotson also gave his resignation. The Church accepted the resignation but allowed him to be Pastor until the first of August 1957, which allowed Pastor Dotson to conclude 20 years of service to the Church. A special retirement service was held for Dr. J. H. Dotson during the month of August; the Church sponsored a *"This Is Your Life"* program; and young Reverend McCutchen was included as one of the speakers for that program.

Upon the retirement of Reverend Doctor Dotson, the Deacon Board began hearing ministers who came as candidates to fulfill the pulpit vacancy, but George Calvin McCutchen was not considered a serious candidate to return as Pastor of Mt. Zion.

> *"Mrs. McCutchen always believed that I would return as Pastor. As for me, I had put it in the Lord's hands. I was open to the leadership of the Divine Spirit and I was willing to be in full agreement with His will."*

The Pulpit Committee of Deacons decided to call a meeting after each pastoral candidate had been heard by the congregation to vote on that candidate. Several strong ministers and good candidates came from far and near for this pastoral position, but all were voted down. There was a group of members, mostly young adults that had organized to vote against every candidate until the name of George McCutchen was placed on the voting ballot.

Wednesday night, October 4, 1957, with Moderator Theodore Rowland presiding, the Church met once again to elect a Pastor. This time the Pulpit Committee reported that since they had been defeated in their selection several times, this night they would not bring in names but would allow names to be brought from the floor. Sister Rosa Drew placed the name of Reverend George Calvin McCutchen in nomination. Two other names were also put into nomination. Since McCutchen's name was submitted first, he would be the last to be voted upon.

When the time came to vote on the young Reverend McCutchen, there was an overwhelming majority "*YES*" vote. The Reverend T. Rowland, Pastor of Mt. Rose Baptist Church was reported as saying—"*This young man wins by a landslide. Suppose we make it unanimous.*"

Even those who preferred someone else was reported to have said "*… well, he is our Pastor too.*" It was decided unanimously that night that Reverend George Calvin McCutchen would be the new pastor of Mt. Zion Baptist Church.

WHEN GOD SAYS NO
Scripture: 2 Corinthians 12:1-11

"For this thing I besought the lord thrice, that it might depart from me. And he said unto me. My grace is sufficient for thee; for my strength is made perfect in weakness. Most gladly therefore will I rather glory in my infirmities, that the power of Christ may rest upon me.

II Corinthians 12: 8, 9

It is very significant that the greatest of all Christian missionaries was a man who bore a physical suffering until his dying day. He had what he called a *thorn in the flesh.*

Just what was his affliction: The scholars have not agreed. Some seem to think that Paul was epileptic. Others venture to say that he suffered from persistent malaria. Still others say, and seem to think, that he had arthritis. In any case, he was a constant sufferer and was greatly troubled.

He was giving his life in the service of the Lord, and it seemed only reasonable that God would take his infirmity away. Three times he says that he sought the Lord, that it might depart from him. But God said no in answer to his prayer, and he carried his affliction to his grave.

I.   **Was Saying No Tot The Apostle Unfair?**

For God to say no to the Apostle Paul, humanly speaking, was a bit unfair. Paul was a spiritual giant. He wrote more of the new testament than any other writer. He started more churches than any other man before his day or since. He laid the foundation of Christian theology. He endured persecutions, and he risked his life a dozen times for the sake of the gospel of Christ.

But, in spite of all that he had done and was still doing; in spite of what he could have been better fitted to; God said no to his prayer of relief, and he went on suffering and serving until his dying day.

A lesser man would have told God that it just isn't fair, or he would have assumed that he needed a new technique to overcome the reluctance of God. But, Paul took his pains in stride saying— *"Most gladly ... will I glory in my infirmities that the power of Christ may rest in me ... "*

From this experience of the Apostle Paul we have to bring ourselves to realize that our way isn't all the time God's way, and that our will isn't all the time His will. It will also help us realize the will of the Lord will and must be done.

II.   **There Are Times When God Does Say No.**

It is said that a man, upon learning that his son was being taken off to the war, took that son and they went to the minister who prayed that the boy might survive the war and return to them safe and unharmed. But, in less than a year, the boy was killed in the midst of the battle. The father, in a fit of rage, ran to the minister's study and said—"Here we have put our trust in God and we asked that he might spare my son. So where was God when my son died?"

The minister just simply informed the man this was one of those times when God had just said no, and he was in the same place that God was when His own son died.

There were many times when we stood around the bed of loved ones and talked to God about their condition. Many times we prayed that God would relieve them of their pains. But perhaps it was one of those times when God just said no and, like the Apostle Paul, our loved ones had to carry their affliction until their dying day.

We have to realize that we are serving a God who spared not his own son. In hours like these we have to pray as God's own son prayed in Gethsemane—"*Father remove this bitter cup if thus thy secret will. If not, content I'll drink it up my calling to fulfill.*"

There are times when we have to say in the language of Job— "*Though He slay me, yet will I trust Him.*"

And we, I say, have to face the fact that there are times when God does say no.

III. When God says No, He Has A Reason.

God knows what is best for us, even as a father knows what is best for his children. When God said no to Paul, Paul was able to put two and two together. When he did that he came up with the idea that his affliction could minister to his family.

Paul says, here I am eloquent in speech; I have a brilliant mind; I'm one of the big wheels in this church; and what is more, I have been one of those proud unbending Pharisees. But, there was a time when I let my pride get in the way of my spiritual insight. There was a time when I let my prejudices stand in the way of my perception of the will of God.

Paul says—God knows me, and He knows what is best for me. God has said no to me, for this thorn can help keep me humble.

Paul knew, as I know, that humility is a difficult virtue when you are riding on the crest of the waves. When one is healthy, wealthy, and popular, it is so easy for one to get the idea that he can get along without God. This thorn was sent to Paul lest he exalt himself above measure.

Paul's thorn served as a perpetual reminder of his spiritual need. He could not cure his own affliction, and even Luke, his beloved physician, tried all types of remedies and failed. So Paul had to face it, God has said no and he will have to bear this thorn and let the power of Christ see him through.

Paul knew what Jesus meant when He said—"*Without me ye can do nothing.*"

For Paul knew that without God's power he could not manage his thorn, but trusting in God he was able to say "*I can do all things through Christ which strengthens me.*"

Without Christ, Paul was whipped before he got started; but, with Him, he was more than a conqueror. Yes, God does say no, but He has a reason for saying no.

IV. **God Links A Yes With Every No.**

Although God does say no, He links a yes with every no. His no is never a bare no. He never says no to our pleas like tired parents who mean that they do not wish to be further bothered. God has linked a YEA with every NAY. He may close up a road, but He will open up another right beside it. Maybe there isn't complete healing, but there is help; and if you look hard enough, you will find healing in that help.

God said to Paul—I'm not going to heal you of your infirmity; I'm not going to remove the thorn from your flesh; but My grace is sufficient for thee. I won't give you too much grace or too little grace, but I give you sufficient grace.

V. **One Thing Can Mean Everything.**

It was just after the civil war, when a man was riding through the bottoms of Mississippi on a train. He looked out over the beautiful cotton fields and said to the gentleman that was riding at his side— "There was a time I could have had that whole plantation for just one pair of boots."

The other man said—"You must have been a big fool sir. Why didn't you take it?"

In reply the man said—"I will assure you that I was no fool sir. I just didn't have that pair of boots."

One thing, I say, can mean everything.

A father reports that he could have saved his son from drowning, if his fishing pole had been just one foot longer. One defective link can ruin a chain; one rotten apple can spoil a barrel; one sin can make man a sinner. That is why Jesus taught one way.

I don't know whether you noticed or not, but the Master lived one life; betrayed by one man; picked up one cross; and marched up one hill. He died one death, as a result of one sin to atone for the world. He was buried in one tomb, and he rose early one morning. He made one announcement saying all power is given unto me both in heaven and in the earth.

One thing can mean everything and one God is big enough for me. My God is so large I can't go around Him; so high I can't go over Him; so low I can't go under Him; so great that the gates of heaven can't contain Him; yet, He is so small that He can take a seat in the stirrup of regeneration and ride in a man's heart.

HOW GOD TAKES CARE OF HIS PREACHERS
Scripture: I Kings 17:1-16

"And the word of the Lord came unto him saying, get thee hence, and turn thee eastward, and hide thyself by the brook Cherith that is before Jordan. And it shall be, that thou shalt drink of the brook; and I have commanded the ravens to feed thee there."

I Kings 17:2-4

"And Elijah said unto her, fear not; go and do as thou has said; but make me thereof a little cake first, and bring it unto me, and after make for thee and for thy son. For thus saith the Lord God of Israel, the barrel of meal shall not waste, neither shall

the cruse of oil fail, until the day that the Lord sendeth rain upon the earth."

I Kings 17:13-14

One October afternoon more than forty-five years ago in the wilderness in the hills of Kentucky, I made the most important decision of my life. I decided to follow Jesus.

I had been brought up in a Christian home. I had attended a little country church and all I ever heard was old fashioned gospel preaching. Many times I heard the preacher say that sin is black, judgment is certain, eternity is long, hell is hot, heaven is happy, and salvation is free. But on that day, I repented of my sins, put my trust in Jesus who died for us all, and I came from that wilderness feeling brand new. I even felt like shouting because I no longer had to lean on myself, I was now leaning on the Lord.

My mother died one year after I got saved, but there were a few things she told me before she crossed to the other side. She said, "The Lord will provide; He will make a way somehow; God will take care of you."

For almost thirty-five years now, I have been blessed to be a member of the Fraternity of Preachers. For 26 years I have been honored to hear folk call me Pastor. I have read a lot of books, preached a lot of sermons, helped a lot of people, and a lot of people have helped me.

I've had a lot of experiences—some have been good, some have been bad. Like most Bible believing Preacher-Pastors, I have been cussed and discussed, and I must confess that there is more to being a Preacher-Pastor than I ever thought it would be. This I know for sure—without the help of God, I would not be equal to the task.

My father went home also to be with the Lord when I was a teenager. While mother and father were here they helped God to take care of me. But since they have been gone now for more than 35 years, God has done it by himself.

I am a witness today that the Lord will provide. On this Sixth Anniversary of your Pastor, I've stopped by here on my way to Heaven to discuss this all import subject—"How God Takes Care Of His Preacher."

I.   **Learn To Lean On The Lord**

Note first of all—happy is the Preacher who learns early how to lean on the Lord. Being a Preacher-Pastor is a teasing, tantalizing task. It is a very serious business. It is a matter of life and death.

We spend more time climbing up the rough side of the mountains than we do resting in the valleys. The cross, instead of a cushion, is the symbol of our faith. Folk lean on us a lot, but even the leaned on must learn how to lean on the Lord.

The Pastor must have faith in God, and it helps if he can have faith in the people of God. Trust must be the watch word of the Gospel Preacher. If you trust Him, you will also obey Him.

Elijah had pleased God because he had led God's people back to the paths of righteousness. He had entered a contest with Ahab's 450 prophets of Baal and had won because his God had answered by fire from heaven. But his faith failed him when after the victory there was a threat upon his life.

Elijah didn't have to run, but he did. Apparently he felt that a good run was better than a bad stand. Now we find him under a juniper tree asking God to take his life.

From exhaustion he fell asleep, and an Angel came all the way from Glory to comfort and care for him. He found a cake and a cruse of water at his head. The Angel told him to eat for he couldn't make it without food for his body. The Journey was too great.

Elijah ate the food the Angel provided, and he went on in the strength of his divine diet forty days, until he came to Horeh—the Mount of God. There in the mountain God spoke to Elijah in a still small voice—don't worry, I will take care of you. You reach up as high as you can, and I will reach down all the way.

Happy is the Preacher-Pastor who learns early how to lean on the Lord.

II.   **Providing For His Preacher**

The second thought is this—God has all kinds of ways of providing for his Preacher.

From Horeh, Elijah was sent by God to the brook Cherith. The scripture reads—*"Then the Lord said to Elijah, go to the east side and hide by Cherith Brook at the place east of where it enters the Jordan River."*

The most important point here is that God did not hide Elijah out of fear of Ahab his enemy, but to show Elijah that God could provide.

Elijah was poverty stricken. He was acquainted with the worse kind of inflation. God needed to show him, in the wilderness, that He would provide. He was told to drink from the brook and eat whatever the ravens brought him. The saints of God who serve our Savior, have nothing to fear.

The prophet obeyed the word of God. The ravens brought him flesh in the morning and bread and flesh in the evening, and he drank from the brook. God provided his Preacher two square meals a day. A square meal is one that you don't have to pay for. It pays to serve Jesus.

I remember when I was the Assistant Pastor at Mt. Zion I was paid $40.00 a week. How did I make it—I was fed by ravens. There were members of the church that God sent to take care of me, such as Mrs. Francis Franklin, Mrs. Alice Latimer, and many others. God has all kinds of ways of providing for His preacher.

III.   **God Does Take Care Of His Preacher.**

The third, and final point is this—God does take care of His preacher, but He does it best through the people he serves.

In the wilderness, God prepared His preacher for "city duty". When the raven failed to bring Elijah's meals and the brook dried up, this was a message from God for Elijah to show himself in the city.

The first person he met was a destitute widow, who was gathering sticks to prepare the funeral meal for herself and her son.

Preachers who stay close to God have divine courage enough to make bold demands on the people of God. Elijah demanded that this widow woman, who had only enough meal for a cake for herself and her son, make him a cake first then fix for the family. I wonder what any of us would have done a situation like that.

This widow decided to take him at his word, and to fix first for her preacher. The reason she was able to do this, she had heard the preacher say—*"Go ahead, don't be afraid. Cook your last meal only fix mine first and afterward there will still be enough for you and your son. For the Lord God of Israel says there will be plenty of flour and oil left in the containers until the time the Lord sends rain and your crops grow again."*

I can very well imagine this widow woman actually hummed a tune as she meditated on the comforting words of the prophet as she obediently fixed a meal for him. She might have hummed a tune like Fanny Crosby's *Blessed Assurance*—especially the verse that goes.... *Perfect submission, perfect delight....* While she worked in the Kitchen, God worked in Heaven.

Saints ought to be glad to fix for God's preacher. While she fixed for her preacher, God fixed for her. The Bible says—as long as the famine remained in the land, her barrel of meal wasted not and her cruse of oil never failed. A last meal marked the beginning of many meals. Don't miss your miracle.

THE GOD APPROVED WORKMAN
Scripture: II Timothy 2:1-15

"Study to show thyself approved unto God a workman that needeth not to be ashamed."

II Timothy 2:15

Serving God and humanity as a preacher of the gospel is truly the highest calling that comes to mortal man. No honor gives me greater satisfaction than to take my place among the wonderful fraternity of preachers. I would rather be with preachers than with any other group in the world.

We are living in an exacting, demanding, critical age and we have a tremendous task to perform. We have a marvelous gospel to preach, a mighty God to serve, and a wonderful world to save.

To my mind the first and greatest work of the man in the pulpit is to preach the Word. If God has called him at all, He has called him to do just that. Almost every other work can be accomplished by laymen and laywomen, but preaching is still the preacher's job.

Nobody tells the pastor what to preach. God is to do that; and, his message is not to be chosen with the view of pleasing the people. He seeks to please God. Beware of being called the popular preacher for this could mean spiritual compromise.

There are many requisites for an effective worker in the Kingdom of God. It is obvious that he should be intelligent, consecrated, and trained. However, there is one requirement that includes all the qualities known to man: we should strive to be the WORKMAN APPROVED BY GOD!

I.   **God Approves The Workman Who Is A Student Of His Word.**

The student of God's Word is the God approved workman. The Bible is now and always will be our textbook. The Bible is a big book. One cannot know it except by diligent well planned study. Study is by no means an easy task; but it is an enjoyable and rewarding venture.

The one whose pulpit ministry is to remain alive, vigorous, stimulating and effective, is the one who keeps on studying week by week and year after year. We must know as much as possible about the Bible but nothing must take the place of a careful study of the book itself.

The God approved workman is a student of God's Word. *"Study to show thyself approved unto God a workman that needeth not to be ashamed."*

II.   **The God Approved Workman Is One Who Works.**

We have a work to do. Several questions may need here to be answered. What is our work? What is the purpose of our work and where does God fit into our work?

Our work is not to invent a new gospel, but to rightly deliver the gospel committed to our trust. Our daily work is more than a job; more than just a way of making a living. Our work is a gift from God. Our work is the King's business.

Workmen who are unskilled, unfaithful, or lazy are never approved by God and need to be ashamed. We are workers—even laborers—together with God. We are laborers together with the carpenter from Nazareth. He makes the blueprints! He oversees! He directs! He does the final shaping!

He takes the imperfect things which we have made and brings the hidden glory out of what oftimes looks like failure. And whoever works with Him need not to be ashamed. God approves the workman who works.

III. **God Approves The Highest And The Best**

God approves the workman who is satisfied with nothing less that the highest and the best. The God approved workman is never satisfied with mediocre performance.

He must concern himself at all times about being God's man in God's place doing God's will. He who stands in the presence of the High and the Highest and accepts the high instead of the highest, even though the high may be holy, that man has sinned.

The preacher must be like the noted musician who was in concert before a large audience. At the close of each selection the crowd would stand and applaud. This man appeared wholly unmoved by the reaction from the crowd but centered his attention toward one seat high in the balcony. When the performance was over and his friends were congratulating him for a job well done, one asked why he appeared unmoved by the emotions of his audience but expressed a concern about one spot in the balcony. His reply was, "*I wasn't worried about the crowd! Seated high in the balcony was my teacher. I was concerned about how well I was pleasing him*"

We shouldn't be too concerned about our popularity with the crowd. Our concern should be to please our teacher who sits in the balcony of Glory, observing our failures and small successes.

The God approved workman studies, works, and is never satisfied with anything less than his best.

A young man was following in his father's footsteps as an artist. One day he decided to paint a picture that would make his father proud. He worked hard on it all day long and at nightfall he had done all that he could do. Yet, he felt that something was wrong. He just couldn't get it right after many attempts. But he put his brushes aside, covered up the canvas and said, "Maybe I will see my errors in the morning."

While he was sleeping, his father lifted the canvas, took up the brushes and gave the painting the finishing strokes, then covered it up again and waited for morning. When his son appeared in the morning and gazed upon the finished work, he made this simple statement, "If I have done my best, then God will take over and do the rest."

My admonition to you as workers for our Lord: When you come to the close of your day, if you have done your best, God will step in and do the rest.

> ## SOMETHING TO HOLD ON TO
> Scripture: Revelations 3:11, Hebrews 10:23

"Hold that fast which thou hast that no man take thy crown.

Revelations 3:11

"Let us hold fast the profession of our faith without wavering, for He is faithful that promised."

Hebrews 10:23

Someone has said, and I'm inclined to agree, unless a man undertakes more than he can do, he will never do all that he can. Let me explain this subject the Divine Spirit has given me to speak from today by sharing a few facts from geography and from history.

The Niagara Falls is divided into two parts; the larger portion on the south side is in Canada, the smaller (northeastern side) is in the United

States and is located 22 miles Northwest of Buffalo, New York. It is 1,000 feet straight across.

The fascination of Niagara Falls for centuries once prompted adventurers to perform many fool hardy acts. History tells us that in the year 1859, a French acrobat, Charles Blondin believing that unless a man undertakes to do more than he can do, will never do all he can, walked the 1,000 feet across Niagara Falls from the United States into Canada on a tightrope, holding a staff the length of a fishing pole in his hand.

When he was asked how he made it over without a single misstep and seemingly without too much fear of falling, his reply was—"It was not easy, but it was not impossible. All I needed was something to hold on to."

What is it that some Christians remain faithful when others aren't?

Why is it that some believers come to church regularly when others do not?

Why is it that some church members consistently pay their tithes and give an offering when others won't?

Well, I believe I've gotten it pretty much figured out. Many of us are willing to stand our ground when Satan challenges us. We are willing to go where we need to go and do what we need to do. It's not easy, but it's not impossible. I would think that our secret is found in the fact that we have something to hold on to.

We refuse to stop reading the Word of God that sustains us. We refuse to surrender the hope that inspires us. We refuse to turn away from the Lord Jesus Christ who loves us, and we can walk on through many dangers, toils and the snares of this dark and benighted world without a misstep and without fear of ailing.

We remember that God is still God. He knows what we are facing. His promises are forever sure. We have something to hold on to.

Permit me to use the remaining moments of time to list and briefly discuss some important things we have that we need to hold on to.

I.   **We Can Hold On To Our Personal Christian Convictions.**

They who fail to stand for something will fall for anything. We can't sell anything we don't believe in. We will never be able to sell

Christ to an unbelieving world, if we don't truly believe in Him ourselves.

The strength of our nation lies in the strength of its religious convictions. Jesus said—*"Ye are the salt of the earth. Ye are the light of the world."*

Some may say you are old fashioned. Some may laugh at your lifestyle. Some may question your sanity and say that you are uninformed and unenlightened. Even so, we need to, and we can, hold on to our personal Christian convictions. We have something we can hold on to.

II. **It Is Important That We Hold On To Our Christian Priorities.**

Secondly, it is important that we hold on to our Christian priorities. Included among them should be the welfare of our immediate families, the making of our lives a Christ like example, the sharing of our Christian experience with others, a special time for devotion and worship, and serving the Lord faithfully and obediently in whatever capacity He so chooses.

It is a known fact if we don't hold on to our Christian priorities we will end up right back where we were. We will forfeit many rich blessings. We will lose what we have already gained. We will bring shame and disgrace to ourselves and to others. We will never know what could have been. We will make the biggest mistakes of our lives and will eventually live to regret the fact that we gave first rate loyalty to so many secondary causes.

It is important that we hold on to our Christian priorities.

III. **Hold On To Our Christian Integrity.**

Next, I would suggest that we hold on to our Christian integrity. If we lose this we will lose our self-respect, lose the confidence of others, and lose the testimony of our faith. We will also lose our opportunities for Christian service. Lets, hold on to our Christian integrity.

Some will think you foolish, but hold on. There are some who will criticize you and endeavor to discourage you, but hold on. Some will mock your determination and will make it somewhat difficult for you, but hold on.

All we need is something to hold on to, and we can hold on to our Christian integrity.

IV.   **Hold On To Our Determination To Live For God.**

Next I would suggest that we would hold on to our determination to live for God.

It may not be easy to climb over every obstacle that will be thrown in your path; it won't be easy to withstand every trial with every disappointment; it won't be easy to handle every apprehension and frustration; but, it can be done. It requires determination. Let's hold on to our determination to live for God.

For nothing else will be sufficient in the time of need. Nothing else will satisfy the hunger of our souls. Nothing else will give you calm in the midst of a crisis. Nothing else will give you courage in the face of opposition. Nothing else will provide the measure of assurance we need in these troubled times. Let's hold on to our faith in God.

Think for the moment of the consequences of letting go. If you let go you will hit the bottom; and that for sure is what everyone does that lets go. If you think things are tough now, just let go and see what happens. If you think your burdens are heavy now, just let go and see how heavy they will become. If you think that your nights are long, just let go and see how much longer they become. If you think your problems are big now, just let go and see how much bigger your problems can get. And if you think that your situation can't get any worse, then just let go and see exactly how much worse it can get. So hold on.

Every child of God, including myself, has at times asked the question— What's the use? Why keep holding on? But it comes back to me like the peal of a bell on a clear night—hold on, it can't be much longer. Hold on—there's a brighter day ahead. Hold on—the battle is just about over. The sun is coming up in the morning. Weeping may endure for the night, but don't give up your faith in God because joy cometh in the morning.

He's shaping us down here so we can fit in up there. Hold to God's unchanging hand.

> ## *PUTTING YOUR BEST FOOT FORWARD*
> ### Scripture: Psalm 1:1

"Blessed is the man that walketh not in the counsel of the ungodly."

Psalm 1:1

One of the most interesting funeral occasions that I have ever heard of was said to have taken place in the state of Alabama. The minister had been called upon to deliver the eulogy at the funeral of a man who had been cantankerous, stingy, vicious, and ungodly. He was one who had the reputation for being the meanest man in town.

As the minister stood by the casket, he talked a little about the love of God; and, when the time came for him to say at least a few personal words about the deceased, he said—"There is not too much good I can say about him. But, I must say, and I think that you will agree, that at times he was worse than he was at other times."

There is a bit of humor in the minister's words, but those words are very descriptive of us as members of the Christian family today. For certainly there are times when we are better than we are at other times. And, there are times when we are worse than we are at other times.

But, it should be the desire of every Christian to maintain an attitude, a spirit, or a disposition that would let the world know that we are ever reaching for the highest and the best. We should be doing as your grandmother and mine used to call—"<u>Putting Your Best Foot Forward</u>".

I. **Not An Easy Job**

Note first of all—this matter of putting your best foot forward is not an easy job. This business of trying to be good carries with it a terrible fight, and no one can rightfully know what a fight it is unless he has tried it.

All of us have our weaknesses, and sometimes we fail to live up to our highest and best. But, believe it or not, the people who make the fewer mistakes and failures are the folk who are headed in the right direction. I think that is why our forefathers and the Christian faith puts so much stress upon our putting our best foot forward.

II.   We're At The Mercy Of Our Feelings

It is all too often that we allow ourselves to be at the mercy of our feelings. Sometimes we do not do our best because we just don't feel like doing our best. Bad people, in my judgment, have no idea how hard it is for good people to be good. There is a war that rages on the inside of a good person continually.

Paul said that *"there is a fight that goes on without, but greater is the fight that goes on within"*. He continued by saying that *".... it is needful that I keep working on myself because the good I would, I do not and the evil I would not, that I do."*

And thus we are encouraged to always be putting our best foot forward for it is the only way that you can keep yourself from being at the mercy of your own feelings.

III.   We Can Expect God To Pour Out His Blessings

Next, we are encouraged to put our best foot forward because it is only then that we can expect God to pour out His blessings upon us.

Someone has truthfully said, "If you give the world the best that you have, the best will come back to you."

If you give God your best, He will have to remove the heaven and the earth to keep from giving you His best. He has said that— *"Before one jot of one title of my word fail, heaven and earth shall pass away."*

Note, when a hard job has to be done, we usually leave it for someone else to do. This is best described by the well known American phrase—"Let George Do It." George, in this case, means anyone beside myself.

There is a legend concerning a king who decided to break his subjects of the habit of letting someone else do what had to be done. Everything was left for someone else to do, and the king decided to teach them a lesson.

One of the roads leading to the town passed by a hillside. Late one night the king went to a narrow spot on this road and scooped out a hallow in the middle of the cart tracks. Then he took a small bundle from under his coat and placed it in the hole in the road. From the hillside he found a huge stone and placed it completely over the hole that he had dug.

The next morning a farmer, driving his cart to town, came upon the stone in the road. Seeing the stone, he murmured something about the people being too lazy to move a stone out of the road, yet he pulled his horses to one side. Almost upsetting the wagon, he passed by the stone leaving it lying right in the middle of the road.

A whole company of soldiers marched down the road and their leader halted them. He ordered them to brake rank and to form a line to march on the other side of the stone. The leader made a little speech to the company about people's carelessness, but no one moved the stone.

Later some peddlers with pack horses passed that way. All of them passed over the stone. One went as far as to stop and look at it, saying in wonder how long has that stone been there, but no one moved the stone.

The days went on and no one moved the stone, although everyone blamed his neighbor for letting it lie in the road. One day the king sent for all who used the road to meet him by the stone. When they were all assembled, he said—"I put this stone here three weeks ago and everyone who passed has blamed his neighbor for not moving the stone."

He then lifted the stone and showed them the hollow place beneath, in which lay a small bag labeled—TO HIM WHO LIFTS THIS STONE. He untied the bag and a stream of golden coins came pouring out.

When you pass the buck, blaming someone else for something that is left undone when you could just as easily do it yourself, you are not putting your best foot forward. I am saying that we are encouraged to ever be putting our best foot forward, for it is only then that we receive the greater blessings from God.

IV.   **There Is Someone Following In Your Footsteps**

Note next, we are encouraged to be ever putting our best foot forward because there is someone following right along in our footsteps. Whatever you do, whether that something is good or bad, someone is using you as their example.

One writer has said that the world of today grew out of the world of yesterday; and the type of world we have tomorrow will depend upon the type of world we have today.

A little boy was once following his father through the wilderness. His father awkwardly caught his foot in a root which almost threw him on his face. His little boy said—"Pay attention where you are walking daddy. Remember I'm walking right along in your footsteps.

So, I'm saying here today, we should be putting our best foot forward because someone else is walking right along in our steps.

V.   **Being Sure You Are Headed In The Right Direction**

Then we are encouraged to put our best foot forward because it is the only way of being sure that we are headed in the right direction. We are all but pilgrim travelers and life moves on for us, either for better or for worse. There are two roads which are opened up to each of us. One is wide and one is narrow. The wide road looks very inviting. Its smooth surface makes traveling seem easy and comfortable. This way, although it seems to offer a full life and a good time, is very deceptive.

Many centuries ago a wise observer of human conduct said "There is a way which seemeth right unto man, but the end thereof are the ways of death."

Thus, you should be ever putting your best foot forward for it is only then can you be certain that you are headed in the right direction.

VI. **Grow Into The Image Of Our Master's Likeness**

Then we are encouraged to be putting our best foot forward for it is only by <u>Putting Your Best Foot Forward</u> that you grow into the image of our Master's likeness. I don't know as we can say that Jesus had any habits or not, but if he had a habit, it was none other than that of putting His best foot forward. When He set His face to go to Jerusalem, He was putting His best foot forward. When He walked into the temple an upturned the tables of the money changers, He was putting his best foot forward.

When they sung that hymn after finishing that last meal, and He went with His disciples to the Mount of Olives, He was putting His best foot forward. When He went a little further in that Garden of Gethsemane, He was putting His best foot forward.

As they marched Him from judgment hall to judgment hall, He was putting His best foot forward. And, had you been able to see Him on His way up Calvary, He would have been easily distinguished from the others who carried their cross, because He was the one that was putting His best foot forward.

While hanging there on the cross, He must have been putting His best foot forward for the first word I heard Him say was in the form of a prayer for His enemies saying—*"Father, forgive them for they know not what they do."*

When He stepped out of that grave on that third appointed morning He was putting His best foot forward, for I heard Him say—*"All power is given unto me both in Heaven and in earth."*

And, as He walked with Cleopas and his friend on that Emmaus Road He was putting His best foot forward for I heard them say—*"Did not our hearts burn within us while that man of God talked with us by the way and unfolded to us the scripture."*

"Blessed is the man that walked not in the counsel of the ungodly...."

CHAPTER IV

"And as ye go, preach, saying, the Kingdom of Heaven is at hand. Behold, I send you forth as sheep in the midst of wolves: be ye therefore wise as serpents, and harmless as doves. For it is not ye that speak, but the Spirit of your Father which speaketh in you."

Matthew 10:7, 26, 20

When George returned to Mt. Zion, it was like stepping into a different river. The three years that he had served as Assistant Pastor, he was responsible only to Pastor Dotson, who made all of the decisions. But returning as Pastor meant the relationship would have to change.

As Assistant Pastor, the people had accepted young George McCutchen and heard his sermons gladly. But now the membership saw a 30 year old country boy as an authority figure; a young man that had never pastored a church was now to take the leading position in Tulsa's second oldest Black Baptist Church; a church that had been torn by the *"1921 Race Riot"* and in need of strong leadership. This was difficult for many to take. Could he do it?

"Although I had never pastored a church, I had learned a lot from my predecessor about working with people. I was grateful to Mt. Zion for giving me the chance."

Being a city missionary, George had committed himself to preach for the Reverend M. L. Paschal at Centennial Baptist Church of Sand Springs, while he was on vacation. He had no way of contacting him, therefore he delayed answering the call for two weeks until Reverend Paschal returned.

Meanwhile, there were members who encouraged him to accept. There were some who told him that he was doing so well as a "Teacher Missionary", that he should stay where he was. Some implied that he was too young, that Mt. Zion needed someone with guts and experience. But young George Calvin McCutchen knew that with God's guidance and help, he could succeed at any task. He accepted the challenge and on January 9, 1958 was installed as Pastor of Mt. Zion Baptist Church.

He gave Southern Baptist a 90 day notice to secure a replacement as Director of the Baptist Educational Center, and once again worked both jobs until the 90 days expired.

The house next door to the church, formerly occupied by the Dotson's was remodeled to be used as a parsonage. After a few months, the new Pastor McCutchen—with his wife, Adelene, and nine month old son George Calvin Jr., moved from the apartment on Rockford to the parsonage next door to the church, and the relationship between Pastor and Church began.

> *"Moving into the church parsonage was a terrible mistake. I was always on the job. It was a big two story house, difficult to heat in the winter and only a water cooler for summer. Also, there were roaches that were hard to get rid of. But, we lived there for five years.*
>
> *"My wife's father, the minister who had married us, came to visit and apparently he was not pleased with our living arrangements. He went back home and sent us the money for a down payment on a home. Shortly thereafter, we moved into the residence where we now live."*

The first ten years were new and different. Reverend McCutchen was the first pastor to keep regular office hours, but Mt. Zion did not have an office in the church. There were several class rooms in the R. A. Whitaker Annex (one was used by the Trustees to count money); there was a phone in the basement that was locked up during the week in a box to keep long distance calls from being made; there was a Pastor's Study; but no Church office.

*"I recall the three and one half years I served as the Assistant Pastor,
I worked in the Pastor's Study but I had to run up and down the
stairs to answer the telephone. Reverend Dotson's philosophy was—
when he was in his study, he was there to do just that. His wife
would take the calls in the parsonage and he would return them
when he was available to talk."*

The new Pastor McCutchen saw as his first task the need to build an
office, install a phone in the Pastor's study and the office, and to hire a
secretary.

The petition was removed between the first two rooms in the Annex;
office furniture was purchased; phones were installed; the typewriter and
mimeograph machine (which had been in the home of members who did
the weekly bulletins and other secretarial duties) were brought back to
the church, and Mrs. Bobbie Thompson (now Mrs. Bobbie Wilson) was
hired as the first Church Secretary.

A Stewardship program was initiated and a Tithing program was
promoted. The annual income began to show a sizable increase.

Pastor McCutchen initiated a monthly donation to the Pastor
Emeritus, Rev. J. H. Dotson, which continued until his death. Then
allocations were made for monthly donations to Mrs. Rebecca Dotson,
the widow of Reverend Dotson, which continued until her death.

After Reverend Dotson's death, Pastor McCutchen encouraged the
establishment of the *"J. H. Dotson Memorial Scholarship Fund"* to help
college students of our congregation continue their pursuit of higher
education. An annual observance is held in March of each year, at which
time Pastor McCutchen preaches his often requested sermon—*"That's
How It Is Down Here—If It's Not One Thing It's Another"*.

Always maintaining close contact with God, and exemplifying the
Spirit of God to all, this new pastor at Mt. Zion spent all of his working
hours, and many hours when he should be sleeping in counseling the
perplexed, performing marriages, preaching funerals, teaching training
courses, administering sacraments, and visiting the sick; holding midweek
prayer services, studying theology books, presiding at board meetings,

and challenging Sunday School teachers; praying with the penitent, comforting the bereaved, and charting the future course of the church.

Along with his visits to the hospitals and nursing homes, Pastor McCutchen often entered the homes of members and others in the community bringing sympathetic understanding to the troubled, words of cheer and loving concern to the ill, tangible assistance to the needy, guidance and direction for the confused, tender rebuke and help to the wayward, and inspiration to the saints. Often he was called upon by elderly members to bring just a quart of milk, a loaf of bread, or a dozen eggs.

MY GREATEST DESIRE FOR THE CHURCH
Scripture: Psalm 37:1-7

"Delight thyself also in the Lord; and He shall give thee the desires of thine heart.

Psalm 37:4

Every man has something he wants, dreams about, and prays for more than anything else in the world. The proud man would have honor. The covetous man would have wealth and abundance. The malicious man would want revenge on his enemies. The homely would have beauty and the barren would have children. Everyone has something he wants more than anything else in the world.

I have many desires. There are many things I want for myself, for Christ and His church. But there is one thing I want for the church more than anything else in the world.

I.   It Is My Desire That Our Church Would Be A Live Church.

If the church is to take its place in the world it must be alive and active. Surely a dead church must break the heart of the Savior who gave His life for it. If the church is to mean anything in the world it must be a spiritual organization. It may be wealthy; it may have thousands of names on roll; it may have a wonderful building; its crowds may overflow every available space; it may even have the strongest preaching and the sweetest singing; but, if it is not alive with the spirit and love of God, it profits nothing. Therefore, a live, spiritual church is my desire.

II.   **It Is My Desire That Ours Would Be a United Church.**

The church can do anything under the sun if it is united. The church today is weak in the face of Satan and the world because it is divided rather than united. I'm praying each day for another Pentecost, for I know that when the day of Pentecost was fully come they were all gathered together in one place and they were all of one accord.

The Psalmist made this observation: *"Behold how good and pleasant it is for brethren to dwell together in unity!"* I want my church to be united!

III.   **My Desire Is That Ours Would Be A Friendly Church.**

Some people who come to the church are lonely. Some of them are strangers seeking fellowship and friendship, and we owe it to the stranger who is within our gates to be friendly.

The story is told of a little boy who attended church on the other side of town from where he lived. He passed several churches on the way to his church. Someone asked him why he went so far to church and he replied, "You know they love a fellow over there."

I wish this could be said concerning our church. A friendly church will attract people miles away. I am desirous that ours would be a friendly church.

IV.   **It Is My Desire That Ours Would Be a Giving Church.**

I'm praying for the day when folk will support God's church in the manner he left for us to support His church—through tithes and offerings. The Lord told us to GIVE money, but we prefer to RAISE it.

A youth approached me the other day and asked me to buy a box of candy. I asked him what organization was sponsoring the sales. His reply was, "A certain church." I asked him "What project?" He answered, "We're going to build a church."

The only way to build a church is through the conscientious giving of tithes and offerings by every member. Folk ought to tithe because Abraham commenced it; Moses commanded it; Jesus commended it; and who are to change it. It is my desire that ours would be a giving church.

V.   **I Wish I Had A Praying Church.**

God's people do not pray enough. Prayer is necessary to our Christian growth. Prayer helps in the time of trouble. Prayer helps in the time of sorrow. Prayer helps one to overcome the temptations of life. Prayer helps one to find God's will for his life. God's people do not pray enough. The church will never progress any more that it prays. My desire is that ours would be a praying church.

- A church that is spiritually alive!
- A church united!
- A friendly church
- A church with each member giving tithes and offerings!
- A praying church!

Yes—these are things I desire for the church, but they do not represent my greatest desire for the church!

What then is my Greatest desire for the church? *"Brethren my heart's desire and prayer to God for Israel is that they might be saved."* Romans 10:1

This is my greatest desire for the church for several reasons:

1.   The salvation of the lost souls of men is the biggest task of the church. The church should be in the saving business. If it is truly doing the task it is assigned all these other things, like a jigsaw puzzle will fall in their proper places.

2.   It's my greatest desire because it was the greatest desire of my Father In heaven. *"God so love the world...."* (John 3:16)

3.   It's my greatest desire because it causes a lot of rejoicing in Heaven. *"I say unto you that likewise joy shall be in heaven over one sinner that repententh, more than over ninety and nine just persons which need no repentance."* (Luke 15:7)

4. It's my greatest desire for the church because being saved gives one the greatest joy.

5. It's my greatest desire because this gives the assurance of eternal life which is man's greatest possession.

YOU CAN MAKE IT IF YOU TRY
Scripture: Revelations 2:8-11

".... Be thou faithful unto death, and I will give thee a crown of life."

Revelations 2:10

While in North Carolina the other week, my host minister, Brother Dennis Epting, and I started talking about some of the experiences we shared together while attending the American Baptist Theological Seminary in Nashville, Tennessee. He brought to my remembrance a tune that was heard very frequently over the radio.

This same tune was humming on every jukebox across the country a year ago. Some of you might remember. It was a tune written and arranged by one Jean Allison entitled—"You Can Make It If You Try"

While we talked together, he reminded me that this was the same Jean Allison who was but a young man running up and down the streets of Nashville when we were there some years ago. We recalled that his father was the owner of the *Bee Line Cab Company* in Nashville, and his family background was one of love and respect.

As a boy, Jean sang only Christian songs. He and four other young men, under the direction of Rev. Richard C. Pope, had a radio broadcast that was heard each Sunday morning. The church of which he was a member gave him little or no encouragement in his singing career, because he was given to sing the modern gospel songs rather than hymns or anthems—which in the language of his minister, "was the only music fit to be sung in a worship service."

Circumstances soon forced the separation of this group and each went his own way. Yong Allison, being ambitious and desirous of using his talent in some manner, turned from the religious and started singing popular songs. His first hit record, which sold over a million copies and brought him to fame and good fortune, was written as a satire against those who ridiculed, those who criticized, and those who made life a misery. The song said to the world—don't give up, and it was entitled "You Can Make It If You Try".

Now, it isn't our aim to appear, in the least, worldly minded; neither is it our aim to bring some of the world into the church. My only desire is to get some of the church into the world. To me there cannot be found a greater philosophy for this business of living than that of Allison's song, "You Can Make It If You Try". This philosophy runs parallel to that of the Spirit who told John there on the Isle of Patmos to write to one of the seven churches in Asia Minor saying *".... be thou faithful unto death, and I will give thee a crown of life."*

I. **There Is No Place On God's Program For Quitters**

This philosophy, *you can make it if you try*, is a good one because it implies that there is no place on God's program for a quitter. It is in keeping with the old statement—"A winner never quits, and a quitter never wins".

Paul, a wise observer of human conduct reminds us that *"... the race isn't given to the swift and neither is the battle given to the strong, but to the one that endureth to the end."*

There is no place on God's program for a quitter. When one enters the Christian race he must be willing to run all the way. There may be more tears of sorrow than there are tears of joy; the pains may be far greater than the pleasures; the investments may be far greater than the returns; the sowing may be love, and the reaping may be hate; the prices for every value received may be high; but, as we journey on toward the finish, we have this assurance that we can make it if we try.

This philosophy implies that God has no place on His program for quitters. The Bible tells us *".... be thou faithful unto death, and I will give thee a crown of life."*

II. **Sets Forth A Secret Of Success**

Note next this philosophy "<u>You Can Make It If You Try</u>" sets forth a secret of success in any pursuit or endeavor. Across the pages of history are many who made their contributions; who rose from failure to success, from seeming defeat to victory, who made it because they tried.

History tells us of one Booker T. Washington who roamed about over the red hills of Alabama. This man had nothing but a dream of Tuskogee Institute, a school to help the common man. Often he went for months without a dime in his pockets, and the world is richer today because he lived. He made it. Yes, he made it because he tried.

Then there is Mary Bethune; One born in the depths of poverty, but one who had faith in God that she could make it. She loved her race and wanted to see them enlightened. She made it. Yes, she made it. She opened Bethune Brookman's College yonder in Florida. She made it, and it was because she tried.

The thing which made Jackie Robinson able to break down the walls of segregation in organized baseball was his ability to be cursed, spit upon, booed and called "nigger", and not fight back. What was his philosophy that served as the controlling factor in his life? Jackie felt that the important thing was that he made it. And he made it, yes, God knows he made it. It was because he tried.

This philosophy sets forth the secret of success in any pursuit or endeavor. "<u>You Can Make It If You Try</u>".

III. **God Has Never Failed Any Of Those Who Believe**

Note, this is a good philosophy for the record reveals that God has never failed any of those who believe in His truthfulness. The entire host of Heaven seem to be fighting on the side with those who believe they can make it.

I should like to think that when Jesus stood facing death on Calvary, He needed a bit of inspiration, for it seemed as though the Father had forsaken Him. So He decided to call up some of the patriarchs and find out their views on how to make it.

First He must have called Abraham. He must have said,—listen Abraham, I must give my life a ransom for many. To do this I must cross the chilly stream of death. Do you think I can make it? Abraham's answer must have been—yes, you can make it. God often commands the difficult. God commanded me one day to leave my native land and to journey into a land that He would show me. I moved out at His command. I journeyed not by sight, but by faith; and I looked for a city whose architect and builder was God. I dwelt with Isaac and Jacob, coheirs with me of the same promise.

Then I like to think He turned to Moses and said—Moses, do you think I can make it? And Moses said—yes, I know you can make it. I stood one day with a towering mountain on both sides of me, with Pharaoh's mighty host trailing along behind me, and the angry Red Sea stretched out before me, and I cried out Lord, please help me to make it. And the Lord said to me—"<u>You Can Make It If You Try</u>".

Wherefore cryeth the Lord unto me, *"stretch forth thy rod, then speak to the children that they may move forward."* And I stretched forth my rod. It was a miraculous power with the omnipresence of the King of Kings and the Lord of Lords. That rod divided the waters and I was able, along with all the children of Israel, to walk through a path God made right trough the sea, with only getting a little mud on our shoes. "<u>You Can Make It If You Try</u>".

I would like to think He called up David and said—David, you were a man after God's own heart. Do you think I can make it? David's reply must have been—yes Lord, you can make it. I was nothing but a little shepherd boy and knew nothing about fighting any army. But there was a big giant by the name of Goliath that had presented a challenge and had frightened the whole army of Israel for forty days and forty nights. I made up my mind that I was going to make it. I gathered a few smooth stones, and I took a little crude sling and hurled just one stone and brought Goliath to the earth with a crashing thud. Yes, "<u>You Can Make It If You Try</u>".

Our confidence in God's faithfulness should make us to be more faithful. The Bible record reveals that God has never failed those who put their trust in Him.

| THE VICTORY MINDED |
| Scripture: I Corinthians 15:50-58 |

"But thanks be to God, which giveth us the victory through our Lord Jesus Christ." (**Moffat Translation**— *"The victory is ours thank God."*)

I Corinthians 15:57

In the darkest hour of the war with Germany when the destiny of civilization was trembling in the balances, the Congress of Allied Women held a meeting in Paris and adopted a ringing slogan. It read—"BELIEVE VICTORY— THINK VICTORY—PREACH VICTORY—LIVE VICTORY". And victory it was, partly because they refused to believe that they were on the losing side.

The reason there are so many failures among men and women in their personal lives is because they have not learned to be "Victory Minded".

The Apostle Paul would have us know that no man has ever failed who was victory minded. We find this trusting Saint in all sorts of trying circumstances. At times he is being stoned; sometimes he is being whipped; and sometimes he is in prison. At times, seemingly, he is forsaken by God and man. But we somehow never find him without a song of gratitude.

He looks out upon hard pressed men and women like ourselves, who are hurrying on to what looks like final defeat, and shouts—we have won, *"The Victory is ours thank God."*

I.   **Hindrances, Obstacles, And Oppositions**

Note first of all, ours is a world of hindrances, obstacles, and oppositions.

A man walking about in a seaport city harbor noticed a pretty little vessel with its white sails shinning in the sunlight. Her sails were spread and there was plenty of wind blowing, but it seemed to make no progress. He couldn't understand why it was not moving on down the river. Were upon he asked the captain, "Why does that little ship fail to move?"

The sailor's reply was a very understandable one. He answered him these words, saying—"Sir, she's anchored."

That is how it is with many of us. There is everything to help us on our heavenly journey, but we make little progress because we are anchored to something here on the earth. That something takes the form of hindrances, obstacles, and oppositions.

There is always something that tends to block the way. A stumbling block; and, sometimes it appears to be too large to walk around or even climb over. There is someone always standing in your sunshine, seeking to cripple your spirit. But I think Paul would have us to know that all we need to do is believe that the right will always triumph over wrong; that truth will always triumph over error; and that nothing can stop one whose faith is anchored in Jesus.

Hear him as he says—"*The victory is ours thank God. Thanks be to God that giveth us the victory through our Lord and Savior Jesus Christ.*"

II.   Afraid Of Dangerous Opposition

When oppositions come, people react in different ways. Some people consider opposition as dangerous and they get afraid. Some people beholding opposition are scared into defeat. People of all races belong to this group.

Some of the Black leaders, or should I say so called Black leaders, in the South (in Georgia and Mississippi) are afraid of White opposition.

Elijah had a servant that was afraid of opposition. While Elijah and his servant slept, enemies surrounded their tent. The servant rose early, pushed back the flaps of the tent and beheld the opposition. Fear gripped his heart and he fell back into the tent, shaking like a leaf on a tree saying, "Master, the enemy is upon us."

The only thing Elijah's servant could see was the opposition. Where upon, Elijah prayed—"*Lord, open the young man's eyes that he might see*." The enemy and the opposition was out there, but God had also stationed outside an invisible army that was fortified with God's spirit that one could chase a thousand, and two could put ten thousand to flight.

Some in the face of opposition get afraid and are frightened into defeat; but, "*The victory is ours thank God*".

III.   When Confronted With Opposition Fret And Complain

Then there is another group, when in the face of opposition, fret and complain. Moses had fretting cry babies in the rear gang, whose belly ached when the bread ran out. This fretting group said—"*Moses has brought us out here to die*". When the Red Sea opposed them they said, "*It would have been better for us to have died amid the flesh pots of Egypt.*"

Some people feel that they are making a contribution by merely complaining and airing their grievances. They fail to realize that fretting kills one's usefulness. Complaining renders one less able to master the obstacles we face. Paul tells us that fretting does not help, and it is useless for "*The victory is ours thank God*".

IV.   When Confronted With Opposition Get Angry And Fight

Then there is another group when confronted with opposition, get angry and fight. The child of God is at his worst fighting. An animal is at his best fighting, but man is at his worse. A lion is vicious and mean. When let loose, he can whip a hundred unarmed men. Man sinks to the level of an animal when he seeks to win his battles over opposition through anger and fighting. How significant are the words of Jesus, "*Peter, put up your sword. He that taketh the sword shall die by the sword.*"

Sometimes it is best to let the Lord do our fighting for us. I am more and more convinced that God and His program is too big to be stopped by any man. There was a poster that gave courage to many a soldier during the war. It was a picture of Joe Louis in combat saying "We are going to win because we are on God's side."

Paul also tells us in so many words that we need not get angry and fight, for "*The victory is ours thank God.*"

V. Surrender In The Face Of Opposition

Then there is another group who, in the face of opposition, surrender. They do a lot of talking until the opposition closes in, then they surrender unconditionally. These tend to travel in a rut. They dig the rut deeper and deeper until they are stopped altogether. To these, Paul would say that we need to have a plan; have a philosophy. Never be satisfied clinging to a vision. There is plenty beyond the hills, but we have to climb them. *"The victory is ours thank God."*

VI. Overcome The Opposition

The last group I want to mention are <u>The Victory Minded</u>. This is the group who, in the face of opposition, overcome.

The first prerequisite for overcoming oppositions is by mastering oneself. No one can master his opposition until he has first mastered himself. Paul was victory minded because he had mastered himself. No man ever failed who was victory minded. Paul asked a question one day, *"Who shall separate us from the love of Christ".* And he brushes all of his foes aside as many flimsily nothings and says, *"I am persuaded that neither death, nor life, nor any other creature shall separate me from the Love of God."* He was victory minded because he had mastered himself.

Some overcome, but how—they overcome by mastering themselves. Some overcome, but how—by inspiration and help from above. Prayer helps to overcome opposition.

The early Christians believed that Caesar had power, but God had all power. The Christian religion at its highest and best never produced cowards and fighters. When the host of hell arise, the Christian religion has never said, hate them down or fight them down. It said—Love them down; pray them down; preach them down; shout them down; pray them down.

"The victory is ours thank God."

> ## ONE MORE NIGHT WITH THE FROGS
> Scripture: Exodus 8:9-10)

"Be so kind as to tell me when you want them to go," Moses said, "And I will pray that the frogs will die at the time you specify, everywhere except in the rivers."

"Do it tomorrow," Pharaoh said.

By right of Devine creation, all people everywhere have the desire to be free. The law of liberation and the spirit of freedom are so much the concern of Heaven that no ruler—no power, structure system, or government can out law or over rule them.

Any attempt to suspend, abridge, or obstruct the basic human rights of any group of people causes Devine intervention. God generally steps in and wrecks any operation which works against His will that seeks to enslave or oppress the helpless and the weak.

For 430 years the wheels of human slavery zoomed in Egypt. But, when the unpaid and unappreciated children of Israel had accelerated the wheels of Egyptian industry to the breaking point of no return, God intervened. God found, commissioned, and told Moses to go tell Pharaoh to "Let My people go."

Moses went down into Egypt and delivered to Pharaoh the only message he had from God. Pharaoh, like most people in a position of power, denied the request, refused to obey God's orders, and tried to find an excuse of not doing what the Lord said do.

It appears that although Moses and Pharaoh did not see eye to eye on this political issue, they were willing to keep their lines of communication in tact. Everyday they debated the issue. Everyday they talked, but could not agree.

Pharaoh, whose heart was already hardened, said to Moses—you must think I'm a fool. These people belong to me. They are my slaves. They are building great pyramids; they are cultivating the crops, building bridges and roads; they are Egypt's greatest assets and I am not going to let them go.

Moses said to Pharaoh—I must warn you that you are dealing with the eternal God. God's not going to come down here personally and make you do right, seeing that you have no do right in you; but God has all kinds of ways of dealing with your kind and making you wish you had been obedient to His orders. All I have to do is go back and tell God that you wouldn't obey.

I. **God Has Many Ways To Whip Folk In Line**

This perhaps should be the first point of the message today. God has many ways to get folk to do what He wants done. God does not have to put you on a sick bed and almost kill you to get you to recognize Him. He does not have to burn your house down, wreck your car, or send your child to jail to get you to know that He is God.

He can just turn nature loose on you. He can make it so cold that you will freeze to death. He can make it so hot that you will burn up.

Moses went back to Pharaoh and told him that God said, "If you don't let my people go, I'm going to turn some frogs loose in the land."

There were ten plagues God sent into the land because of Pharaoh's disobedience. This time he sends frogs. These little agile animals forced their way everywhere.

God has many ways to whip folk in line. God has many ways of getting folk to do what He wants done.

II. **The Inconvenient, Irritating, Tormenting Power Of Frogs**

Pharaoh wouldn't listen to Moses and there were frogs everywhere. There were frogs in the bedrooms. The Egyptians would pull their sheets back to retire for the night and frogs would jump out their beds.

There were frogs in their kitchens; open the refrigerator and frogs would jump out. There were frogs in their ovens; frogs in their cooking utensils; frogs everywhere. Every home in Egypt was filled with frogs. There were frogs in every corner of the land. These frogs were more inconvenient, tormenting, and irritating than they were dangerous. Few folk realized how strong God is.

Napoleon was a strong general. History tells us he marched across Australia. Alexander the Great was a strong general. At the age of twenty he had conquered all the nations around him and wept because he had no more nations to conquer.

Louis Patton, Eisenhower, George Washington, and Andrew Jackson all made a name for themselves in history as being great generals. All these men were great, but none of these men had the power to put together a frog army. God is the only general that could do that. If He tells the frogs to get together, they will do just that and they will come and fight for Him. Frogs have an inconvenient, irritating, tormenting power.

III. Folk In Their Right Mind Don't Want To Live With Frogs

Note next that folk in their right minds don't want to live with frogs for long.

Do you know what a frog is? He's a strange creature. He's the only animal that can stand up and sit down at the same time. He reminds you of folk who can never take a positive stand on any issue.

The frog has very little body; he's mostly eyes and legs. He reminds you of folk who are gifted at seeing others faults and jumping in places and in folk's business where he doesn't belong.

Then there is a kind of frog that makes a lot of noise. There can be but one frog in a pond and you would think there were a dozen. Some say he's just praising his own pond. I personally believe he's just making a lot of unnecessary noise

These frogs were so many, so irritating, and so tormenting that folk in their right minds do not want to live with frogs for long.

IV. Some Folk Put Off For Tomorrow What They Should Do Today

Observe that some people have the tendency to put off until tomorrow what they should do today. Pharaoh didn't like these frogs any more than anyone else did.

God told Moses, "Tell Pharaoh if he lets my people go I will cause all the frogs to die except those in rivers and other places they ought to be. And, I will do it whatever time he specifies."

Pharaoh said to Moses, "Go back and tell your God I will let them go on tomorrow. I'm not going to let them go today. I want to spend one more night with the frogs."

There is a tendency in some people to do tomorrow what they really should do today.

This brings me to the final thought of this message—

V. **The Danger Of Spending Another Night With The Frogs**

The frog is a metaphor of sin. It is dangerous to keep putting off right to do sin, evil, and wrong. We also have a picture here of a lost man outside the ark of safety.

God has told us that the wages of sin is death, but the gift of God is eternal life. You can quit before pay day.

Trouble, fear, drought, bankrupts, sickness, burdens, trials and tribulations—all these things represent frogs. You don't have to live with these things. You may be lost in sin, but you can claim salvation today in the name of Jesus.

The Holy Ghost says, "Today". You can do that right now. You don't have to spend another night with the frogs. It is dangerous to entertain the idea of spending one more night with the frogs.

You hear folks say I'm going to get right tomorrow. What they are really saying is—one more night with the frogs. They are counting on tomorrow and they should not do that.

The only one we can count on is God, for He owns all of our tomorrows.

I should not close this message until I tell you what to do when that irritating, tormenting frog of sin gets into your life.

Don't call the City County Health Department; don't call the Orkin Pest control man; get on the Royal telephone and call 1-1-1. One for the Father—One for the Son—One for the Holy Ghost and ask to speak to Jesus. Tell Jesus "I got some frogs in my life and I want you to get them out." Just leave it to Jesus and He will move all the frogs out of your life.

Anybody here know anything about Him? Do you know Him? Somebody called Him a way maker; somebody called Him a bridge over troubled waters; somebody called Him the lily of the valley; someone said He is a way out of no way, bread when you are hungry, water in dry places, a friend when all others have gone.

One thing frogs do not like is prayer. Start praying and frogs will start hopping away. Take your burdens to the Lord and leave them there.

NOTE: Each year on the 2nd Sunday in March, Pastor McCutchen delivers his Annual Sermon "If It's Not One Thing It's Another". Over the years the sermon has taken on different titles with different slants on the same message. This is a copy of the message that was delivered by Dr. McCutchen in March 2007.

WHAT CAN WE DO WHEN TROUBLE COMES
(IF IT'S NOT ONE THING IT'S ANOTHER)
Scripture: Psalm 34:19, Psalm 121:1

"Many are the afflictions of the righteous, but the Lord delivers him out of them all."

Psalm 34:19

"I will lift up my eyes to the hills from whence comes my help."

Psalm 121:1

Have you ever had bad days when you simply could not win? One fellow was driving home from work one evening and heard a radio announcer suggest to his listeners that they surprise their mates when they got home. "When you arrive for dinner," he said, "instead of growling something like 'when will dinner be ready; why not surprise your wife with a little gift?"

The man thought that sounded like a good idea, so he stopped along the way for a bouquet of flowers and a box of candy. Instead of driving into the garage, he went up to the front door and rang the bell. His wife opened the door; saw him standing there with a radiant smile on his face, holding out his gifts to her. But she declared crankily to him—"Well if this don't beat it all? Listen Buster, the baby has colic, the washing machine is broken again, and Junior got into a fight at school today and got expelled. Now, as I may have expected, you make my day perfect by coming home drunk!"

Trouble—no one likes it, but no one is very successful in avoiding it. In one way or another trouble seems to be a fact of life. Trouble has no age preference. It invades the life of a young person as well as the old. Trouble has no respect for gender, race or social circle. Trouble invades the life of the rich and the famous. Trouble also visits the unknown and the poor. Trouble—one product in which the supply exceeds the demand.

Trouble is as inevitable as a rainy day after you have washed and polished your car. It is also a penalty we all must pay, because we all belong to the human race. That's how it is down here—IF IT'S NOT ONE THING—IT'S ANOTHER.

Tonight I want to attempt to answer a very important question— "WHAT CAN WE DO WHEN TROUBLE COMES?"

"Grit your teeth and bear it" is the philosophy many would suggest when trouble comes. For trivial matters, especially troubles of our own making, this might work.

If you have lived as long as I have, you realize that there is good trouble and bad trouble. But my message tonight is to realize—that a dark shadow can fall across the path of any one of us at any time. But keep this in mind—there is no dark path in your life or mine that God can't shine His light upon.

The Psalmist—tells us we can give our problems to God. He says *"I will lift up mine eyes to the hills from whence comes my help; my help comes from the Lord who made the heaven and earth."*

My first thought is this—If you find a path that has no trouble, you will also find that it leads to nowhere. Paul Harvey once said, 'you can always tell when you are on the road to success—it is up-hill all the way.'

Trouble, like crosses, comes in all sizes. As soon as you get your car paid for—it's falling apart.

- If it's not the tires—it's the brakes.

- If it's not the transmission, it's the wheels that need an alignment.
- Get your car problems solved—house problems begin. The roof leaks.
- Get the roof replaced—then you discover that termites are eating away the foundation.
- By the time the taxes are paid—the insurance becomes due.
- If it's not the furnace that needs fixing—it's the compressor in the air-conditioning unit that needs to be replaced.
- If it's not the paint—it's the plumbing.

If it's not one thing—it's another.

Our bodies cause us trouble. They may appear to be as beautiful as the starry skies, but they are as fading as a summer flower.

- If it's not your lungs—it's your kidneys.
- If your hair is not falling out—your teeth need fixing.
- If your back is not hurting—your feet are giving you trouble.
- And if arthritis don't stop you from walking—laryngitis will stop you from talking.
- If you don't have a cold—you are burning up with a fever.

If it's not one thing—it's another.

As for life at the church—

- if it's not the program—it's the budget.
- Get the auxiliaries to functioning properly—trouble is found somewhere else.
- When the shepherd is forced to speak well of the wolf, the sheep are in serious trouble.

If nobody knows the troubles you've seen—you don't live in a small town. If, in this life, you find a path that has no trouble you will also find that it leads to no-where. That's how it is down here—*if it's not one thing—it's another.*

So much for the trouble. The question I planned to answer during the second half of this message tonight is—"<u>WHAT CAN WE DO WHEN TROUBLE COMES</u>?" Here are four suggestions to allow God's help to reach us.

I. **Try To View Trouble Objectively**

First—I would suggest that we try to view trouble objectively. Establishing a proper perspective is indeed a difficult task. It is important that you would ask some questions of yourself. Most of the trouble is of the minor nature we have brought on ourselves. God has equipped us with a sense of humor. We ought to use it to take a good look at ourselves.

It takes two things to blow down a tree. A heavy wind outside and rot and decay inside.

So it is with man. The winds of adversity may cause him to bend, but if he is strong and vigorous within, he will arise and grow to new heights after the storm passes. He knows not his own strength who has not met with adversity. To answer the question—what to do when trouble comes?—First, try to view the trouble objectively.

II. **See Trouble As God's Opportunities**

Secondly, when troubles come, we must see them as God's opportunities. We must not wallow in self pity asking why did this have to happen to me. We ought not to bristle in resentment, nor brood over our troubles. We ought not fret or complain. Trouble will make you and I bitter or better. Our God is a sovereign God. He overrules all things for the ultimate good of those who love Him.

The gem cannot be polished without friction nor the child of God cleansed without adversity. Here's a parable of the over-comer. The parable is told of an old dog that fell in the farmer's well. After assessing the situation, the farmer sympathized with the dog and decided that neither the dog nor the well was worth saving. He decided to bury the dog and put him out of his misery.

The farmer began shoveling dirt into the well. The dog was hysterical. As the farmer began shoveling dirt on his back, he would shake it off and step up. He kept shaking it off and stepping up—and at last could step out of the well.

No matter how painful the blow or how distressing the situation—remember the problem designed to bury us can benefit us, if we shake them off and step out of the well we find ourselves in. When trouble comes see them as opportunities.

III. **Some Troubles Not Always Meant For Us**

Here's another thought. When trouble comes, remember God takes us through a multitude of experiences that was not meant for us at all—they are meant to make us more useful in His hands. Troubles not only develop character, they reveal it.

IV. **Look Outside Ourselves For Strength**

Also when trouble comes, we must look outside ourselves to the source of all our strength. When the Psalmist asks, from whence cometh my help, his answer is "my help cometh from the Lord."

There are three ways God's help comes to us. First, it is by **PRAYER.** Man is never as tall as when he kneels before God—never as great as when he humbles himself before God. And the man who kneels to God can stand up to anything.

Reverend Doctor Jesse Jai McNiel tells the story of the time he visited his mother, who was dying of Cancer. As he walked into the hospital room and saw his mother lying in her sick bed dying, he asked—"Mother, are you praying?"

Her answer was "I am not. A long time ago when the blood flowed warm in my veins, I prayed then, now I can **TRUST.**"

I've found that the greatest power in this world is the power of prayer.

Another way God helps get to us is by **BIBLE STUDY.** Growth in grace and in knowledge of the Lord can be obtained only through in-depth Bible Study.

These words of caution when troubles come "Keep traveling this road—when you reach and cross that river—your road going to change."

CHAPTER V

*"Not that we are sufficient of ourselves to think anything
of ourselves but our sufficiency is in God."*

II Corinthians 3:5

Although Pastor McCutchen was greatly involved in the community, the district, and the national work his duty and dedication to Mt. Zion never went without his full attention. He was in the office on a daily basis, and he was in the pulpit preaching the two Sunday services each week. It was a rare occasion when Pastor McCutchen would be out of the pulpit for any reason.

The records show that during the past 50 years under Pastor McCutchen's leadership, over 1200 new members joined Mt. Zion. Pastor McCutchen has baptized over 500 members, married over 150 couples, conducted more than 450 funerals, and dedicated over 250 babies. (We say "over" because there were at least five years of his ministry that records were not properly kept.)

Pastor McCutchen has been a guiding force in the lives of so many young ministers. There has been an array of Associate Ministers who have come through Mt. Zion during Pastor McCutchen's years at the Church. He has worked with them, counseled them, and encouraged them as they set forth as Pastors of their own churches; many of whom have gone on to be outstanding pastors of larger churches around the county.

As of this time Mt. Zion has ten Associated Ministers assisting in the various work areas of the church—Dr. James Norwood, Dr. Laura Norwood, Rev. Wilburn Ware, Rev. Maurice Hatton, Rev. Danny Geeter, Rev. Thomas Humphrey, Rev. George McCutchen, Jr., Rev. Melvin Murdock, Rev. Ann Johnson, and Rev. Wilma Bonner.

In 1980 Reverend Robert Marshall was hired as Assistant Pastor to help in Mt. Zion and to be there when Dr. McCutchen participated in a preaching mission in the Philippines. Reverend Marshall resigned this position in 1982, to pastor his own church in North Tulsa.

Mt. Zion's accomplishments under Pastor McCutchen's dynamic leadership have been numerous and varied. The church has grown numerically and spiritually. The congregation burned an old mortgage on the building, purchased a new piano for the fellowship hall, purchased additional office equipment, refurbished the grand piano in the sanctuary, installed new central heat and air throughout the church, installed new glass doors for the front entrances of the church, furnished the ladies lounge, put cushions on the pews, carpets on the floors, covering for stain glass windows and remodeled and modernized the kitchen and fellowship hall.

The construction of the I-244 Expressway and Urban Renewal caused the entire community around the church to relocate. This caused a decline in Sunday School and Worship attendance. There was very little activity in the community, but Mt. Zion prayed and stayed. Under Pastor McCutchen's strong leadership Mt. Zion endeavors to be a servant of its members and of the community.

Mt. Zion also purchased additional property for parking, installed a stair glide for handicapped members and purchased transportation for members needing rides to church activities and worship services.

In 1984 Mt. Zion engaged in a $550,000.00 bond program. The funds were used to remodel the choir stand and refurbish the pews in the sanctuary; to change the Fellowship Hall in the basement into a study hall dedicated to the memory of the late Dr. J. H. Dotson; and to build the Family Life Center, which houses the administrative offices, a library, study rooms, showers in both the Women's and Men's Restrooms, a commercial kitchen and combination basketball court, stage, and dining hall. The Family Life Center (renamed the G. Calvin McCutchen Family Life Center) has been a catalyst in the community for banquets, weddings, and other activities.

In 1994 Mt. Zion completely remodeled the sanctuary; set up a computer lab in the Dotson Hall; later cleaned the outside of the building to make Mt. Zion an enhancement to the area; and purchased a new Grand Piano for the sanctuary.

Mt. Zion initiated a *"Help Project"* that continues to operate giving food, clothing and support to the needy; an *"Evangelistic Team"* that strives to reach the lost for Christ; and a *"Golden Respite"* group that meets twice weekly with the senior citizens, giving them an outlet for fun, fellowship, and meals.

Members of Mt. Zion have created *"Zion Productions"*, a community theater group that presents outstanding Christian plays. Recently Mt. Zion started a *"Prayer Ministry"* that set up a call center in the Annex with a prayer hot line for those in the church or community that need help.

In order to reach the younger people of the community, Mt. Zion started a **Children's Church and Youth Ministry** with Reverend Ann Johnson as Youth Minister and Coordinator. In 2006 Reverend Damien Bonner came to Mt. Zion and assisted Reverend Johnson in the youth ministry.

An Alcohol Anonymous organization, Meals on Wheels, and Physical Therapy Classes of Rogers University at Tulsa are presently housed in the church facility.

With the growing of the downtown Tulsa area, and the campus of OSU at Tulsa, Mt. Zion seized the opportunity to purchase several acres of land on North Apache, just in case Mt. Zion was crowded out and needed to rebuild the church. This move has not become necessary. Mt. Zion remodeled one of the buildings on this property and opened the *"Heavenly Treasures Books and Novelties Bookstore"* on December 13, 2006

Mt. Zion is a church where the people have *"a mind to work"* and, with the Lord's guidance and help, and under the leadership of Pastor McCutchen, Mt. Zion continues to move forward in the faith that built, is building, and will continue to build a greater church.

George Calvin McCutchen, a young man just out of seminary and college and *One of the Whosoevers*, stopped by Mt. Zion in 1953. During the past 50 plus years, he has been a dedicated advocate for spreading God's word and teaching the gospel. He has been a servant and an inspiration to the congregation. He has made and is continuing to make a tremendous impact on the church and its membership.

THE TEN MOST WANTED PERSONS IN THE CHURCH (Part I)
Scripture: Acts 2:47

"And the Lord added to the church, daily those who were being saved."

Acts 2:47b (NKJV)

The words of the text the Divine Spirit has prompted me to talk from today and during my next preaching moments, tells us what happened following the Day of Pentecost, when the New Testament church was established. The Bible says the members were filled with the Holy Spirit, there was an atmosphere of oneness, togetherness and unity; there was also a spirit of caring, compassion and love. God was glorified, Christ was magnified, the devil was horrified and as a result—God added to the church daily those who met the requirements for salvation.

I particularly like the phrase which says, "The Lord added to the church." I would like to believe that all who hold membership here were added by the Lord. Nothing gives me a greater joy than to open the doors of the church and see folk respond to the Invitation, walk the aisle and express the desire to become a member, who will assume their share of responsibility and help carry the load the Lord has assigned to us here. When that happens, I know they didn't just join the church—the Lord added to the church.

Today I want to borrow a phrase from the FBI. Every now and then, in public places, especially in government buildings there is a list of the **TEN MOST WANTED CRIMINALS**. That list changes from time to time. The FBI's most wanted list contains the names of some of the most notorious people of the world, who are armed and dangerous, a menace to society, who are a threat to those of us who are labeled peace-loving, law-abiding citizens.

But my most wanted list is quite different. It does not change from time to time. It is the same today as it was back in the first century when God added people to the church. Instead my most wanted list contains no notorious criminals, it contains none who are a menace to society, but those who will be a blessing to and help advance the Kingdom of our Christ. I want to invite them to become a part of the membership and become a laborer in the vineyard of our Lord.

I have a list of the **Ten Most Wanted Persons in the Church**. I'll only mention five of them today and the other five when I stand before you again—lest, I keep you too long. Here's my list.

I.   *Brother True Believer*

I think you will agree with me when I say, the Church is in need of True Believers. Belief is the heart of Christianity. Belief is the foundation upon which our salvation is built and stands.

The word "believe" occurs more than 300 times in the sacred scriptures. The importance of believing has never been stated more eloquently than in John 3:16—"For God so loved the world etc."

In Paul's letter to the Romans he says in no uncertain terms that belief is essential to salvation; that "*if thou shalt confess with thy mouth the Lord Jesus and shalt believe in thine heart that God hath raised him from the dead thou shalt be saved.*"

Without a doubt, belief in God—belief that Jesus Christ died on a Roman cross, was buried, that He got up from the grave on that third day. These biblical truths are the foundation of the Christian Religion. The first name on my most wanted list in the church is Brother True Believer.

II.   **Sister Willing Worker**

The church cannot thrive and survive without Sister Willing Worker, for she works not for personal glory but for the Glory of her God. She works not because she loves the spot-light but because she loves the Lord. She works not to have people singing her praises, but so that people will sing praises to our God.

Sister Willing Worker does not have to be begged, coerced, bribed or threatened before she works. She volunteers to do the job. Sister Willing Worker has a theme song that expresses her willingness to serve. It goes like this—*"Count on me, count on me. For loving hearted service glad and free—count on me. Count on me, count on me—oh blessed Savior—count on me."*

Sister Willing Worker is the second on my most wanted list.

III.   Brother Unquestioning Faith

This church is desperately in need of more members with Unquestioning Faith. The Bible says in no uncertain terms that *"without faith it is impossible to please God."* I understand the word impossible—to put it another way, "It ain't no way you can please God without faith." We get on God's nerve when we demand too many answers.

We need faith like Abraham, when he left home without a road map. We need faith like Moses had when they got to the Red Sea; faith that causes one to say, "Stand still and see the salvation of the Lord."

We need that kind of faith that the three Hebrews had that will say to King Nebuchadnezzar who set up his golden image. We may burn, but we will not bow—the God we serve is able to deliver even us from the burning fiery furnace.

We need men today who are willing to say—I'll go Lord if I have to go by my self. Wherever you lead Lord, I'll go. Brother Unquestioning Faith is the third on my most wanted list.

IV.   Sister Spirit Filled Witness

Truly we need more people who truly know the Lord and who aren't afraid to tell others what they know about Him. We need folk who have been lifted out of the "Guttermost" and raised to the "Uttermost" and aren't ashamed to tell the world about it. We need some spirit filled women like the woman of Samaria, who after meeting Jesus, left her water pot and ran all the way up town saying "Come see a man who told me all the things I ever did."

The fourth person on my most wanted list is Sister Spirit Filled Witness.

V. **Brother Impeccable Character**

I'm looking for someone who is honest, decent, and truthful—a person with integrity. This person doesn't have to be perfect. But it would help a lot if he was a composite of many Christian virtues. I'm looking for that person who has put away many of the vices they used to do in the past. Who believe with the Apostle Paul who said, *"Therefore if any man be in Christ, he is a new creature, old things have passed away, behold all things have become new."*

I'm looking for that person who has been washed white in the blood of the lamb.

I have come now to the half way point of my Most Wanted List. I wonder if anyone here today has made a perfect score. I will mention five more the next time I stand before you.

Before I go to my seat may I repeat—these are the kinds of people whom the Lord added to the church after the Day of Pentecost. You can understand—they were filled with the Holy Spirit—all on one accord and they were in one place. They had put aside their personal agendas. They had gotten their acts together, and when they did—the Lord added to the church daily those that were being saved.

THE TEN MOST WANTED PERSONS IN THE CHURCH (Part II)
Scripture: Acts 2:47

"And the Lord added to the church daily those who were being saved."

Acts 2:47b (NKJV

One of the greatest problems of our day is the identity of the church. Three questions often asked—What is the church? Who belongs to the church? How can we find the church?

One thing we must all agree on is—the church is not a building, not a program, not an organization—the church is people. The church is composed of God's redeemed people in whose hearts Jesus Christ reins and rules.

During the past week I borrowed a phrase from the F.B.I. found in public places, especially Federal Buildings—**The Ten Most Wanted Criminals**. And I discussed—Part One of the Ten Most Wanted Persons in the Church.

I stated that the government's list changes from time to time—but the church's most wanted list remains the same. If we are going to follow the Lord, we must do it on His terms and not ours. And my text reads—*"And the Lord added to the church daily those who were being saved."*

Of the Ten Most Wanted People in the Church, I listed five:

1. *Brother True Believer*
2. *Sister Willing Worker*
3. *Brother Unquestioning Faith*
4. *Sister Spirit Filled Witness*
5. *Brother Impeccable Character*

I only got half way through my list. Well, lets look at the next five.

I.   Sister of Brother Cheerful Giver

Ah, what a joy it is to see people who seem to enjoy giving freely of their time, their talents, of their means—most of all *themselves to the Lord to benefit His church. The Bible says* "The Lord loves a cheerful giver." This is said for the good of the giver.

When you give grudgingly, the church may benefit from your gift but you don't get any heavenly benefit for yourself. I've heard ministers ask folk to give until it hurts. I'd rather be asked to give until it stops hurting. When one's heart is in the right place, you will give until it feels good. Jesus left on record how He felt about giving when He said, *"It is more blessed to give than to receive."* (Acts 20:35)

Church folk need to learn that money can't buy everything. Granted, money has power. But it also has weaknesses. For instance, money can buy land, but not love; bonds but not brotherhood; gold but not gladness; silver but not sincerity; hospitals but not health; condominiums but not character; houses but not homes; timber but not truth. Money can purchase commodities, but not comfort; ranches but not righteousness; ships but not salvation and hotels but not heaven.

To save your money you must share it; to love it is to lose it, and to invest it forever you must put it in things eternal. Therefore, one of the Ten Most Wanted people in the church is Brother or Sister Cheerful Giver.

II. **Brother Daily Bible Reader**

When you pray every day, you are talking to God; but when you read your Bible daily, God has a chance to talk to you. When you pray daily and fail to read the Word daily, you are monopolizing the conversation.

Can you imagine holding a conversation with God and not allowing Him to get in a single word? With all of His accomplishments I'm sure He has something to say. Someone put it like this—"Read your Bible every day, praying while you read it. It will guide you all the way, if you only heed it." The only way we can do better is to know better and the only way we can know better is to daily read and study God's Word. So, the seventh person on my Most Wanted List is Brother Daily Bible Reader.

III. **Sister Pleasing Personality**

Did you realize that your personality is everything about you which makes you the person you are. The Lord, the church, even the Pastor, needs folk working in the church with a pleasing personality.

The way you walk, the way you talk, the way you smile, the way you live, the way you give and a long list of a lot of things makes for a pleasing personality. It's a wonderful thing to see someone in church with a composite of these virtues and qualities.

There are folk even in church who will captivate you by their presence. On the other hand, there are folk when you see them coming, you know they are not going to make your day—rather they are going to break it.

Some people have the knack for bringing out the best in other people, and there are folk who bring out the worst. Oddly enough, I've seen very few ugly Christians, because what's on the inside has a way of showing up on the outside. Ah, what a blessing it is to have a pleasing personality. That's number eight on my Most Wanted List.

IV. **Brother Childlike Humility**

I'm looking for someone who can walk with Kings and not lose the common touch. I'm looking for someone who fails to stay on any ego trip, someone who is not wrapped up in his or herself. It doesn't take too much to do this for some people.

One month ahead in rent, ten cents above breakfast money. Don't let them get two chickens in a pot and ten in a freezer—and they will call themselves a humble servant. When one finds himself or herself boasting about their humility—they just lost it.

Only if man strikes rock bottom in the sense of his own nothingness will he strike the Rock of Ages. Humility is to make a right estimate of oneself. Brother Childlike Humility is number nine on my list.

V. **Sister Endless Love**

Endless love is closely related to that kind of love which Jesus had when He went to Calvary. Endless love does not depend upon the attitude of the other person involved. Endless love keeps on loving when others become unlovable. Endless love makes you treat your enemies with the same type of kindness you display with your friends. Endless love makes you bless them that curse you and pray for them which despitefully use you. Endless love makes one turn the other cheek and go the extra mile.

I have mentioned The Ten Most Wanted Persons for God's Church today. What a blessing will we be to the community when we allow this list to become a reality in our congregations? What do you suppose would happen on a given Sunday if some of those who have been doubting would be converted into true believers?

- And then some of those willing watchers would become willing workers?

- And what would happen if some dry, dehydrated, sophisticated worshipper would catch on fire and become a true believer?

- And what would happen if those misers and penny pinchers would become tithers and cheerful givers?

- And what if all those proud, arrogant people would come out of their ivory towers and begin practicing childlike humility?

- And suppose our congregation would be attacked by a virus of endless love?

There would be another Pentecostal experience. The Lord would add so many to His church that we would not be able to count them. You see, Satan would have no place in a church like that. We could put the devil on the run.

We would sing and keep on singing—Victory is mine, Victory is mine, I told Satan get thee behind, Victory today is mine.

HOW TO GET OUT OF HELL
Scripture: Jonah 2:1-2

"Then Jonah prayed unto the Lord his God, out of the fish's belly, And said—I cried by reason of mine affliction unto the Lord. And He heard me, out of the belly of hell, I cried and thou heardest my voice."

Jonah 2:1-2 (KJV)

I am of a strong opinion that the religious experience of our generation has been seriously impoverished as a result of our tragic failure to believe in the haunting reality of Hell. Claiming to be intellectually superior to our fore-parents, we have dismissed the doctrine of the brimstone and the fiery pit as nothing more than a frightening, fabricated fairy tale. A silent consensus that views hell as an invention of the pulpit has emerged.

The word has been whispered from person to person, from pew to pew and from place to place that Hell is an allegory invented by pulpiteers of the other days for the purpose of frightening us out of enjoying the pleasures of life—and devoting our time to serving the Lord. Yet, as neat and convenient such an explanation may sound, there is no escaping the fact that Hell is more than a scare tactic. But whether we believe it or not, hell is a fact of the after life. Hell is a certainty. Hell is a reality.

When our forebearers spoke of heaven and hell, we ridiculed them and accused them of being other-worldly. But other worldly or not, at least they knew that no matter who you are in this world, you reap what you sew—you get what you give—what goes around comes around—what goes up will surely come down—that a person can experience the fiery fingertips of hell by experiencing the consequences of one's own evil action.

The religious experience of our time is short changing us because it is missing the grave accent of the judgment of God. It is telling us about the boundless blessings of God and about the precious promises of God, but it is not telling us that "the soul that sinneth, shall die." We are not taking seriously the judgment of God and the consequences of our own evil actions. Despite all our positive thinking, the devastating effects of sin and the scorching proof of hell are still around us.

Some of us have avoided an early grave and missed a whole lot of hell in life because we were taught that "the fear of the Lord is the beginning of wisdom." No matter what we may say Hell is just a damnable, unfortunate set of circumstances that we create for ourselves. When we live our lives with no regard for the judgment of God, we're headed for Hell. No there is no need to think of hell as only an experience in the afterlife; hell is a fact of life. (ELAB)

All across our world there are conditions that trap and torture human life in the red hot flames of Hell. It is Hell to have to walk dangerous streets overcrowded with dope fiends, cut throats and back stabbers. It's hell to live in a land of so-called opportunity and I can't find a summer job. Hell is a situation from which there seems to be no exit. No matter what the circumstance we always need a way out. Therefore—the Divine

Spirit has prompted me to talk from this very important subject *HOW TO GET OUT OF HELL.*

My first thought is this—no matter how you get in hell, Jonah will tell you that there is a way out.

Some people are on a two hour furlough from Hell and they come to church looking for a way out. Some people are AWOL from hell and they slip away to the church looking for a way out. The good news is no matter how you get in hell, there is a way out. Ask Jonah. He landed in hell, but he will tell you that there is a way out.

As a prophet of God, Jonah should have known that hell was his destination when he disobeyed God's orders and tried to do things his way. You will recall that an angel came and announced to Jonah that he was to be the guest preacher at the first city wide revival service to be held in the sinful city of Nineveh. But Jonah hated the Ninevites and didn't want to go because he didn't want them to be saved. Jonah said to himself, "How I love to preach and I have a message them Ninevites need to hear—but if God plans to save them—He's going to get Himself another preacher. I'm not going to Nineveh. I'm going to take me a vacation in Tarshish." So Jonah went down to Joppa, his desired vacation spot, but ended up in Hell.

A ticket to hell costs an awful lot. I can't tell you how much it costs. But I can tell you this—it costs more than most folk can afford to pay. The Bible says—Jonah paid a fare to Tarshish to get away from God. I need to tell somebody today, I don't care how good it looks or how popular the best spot is, if you trying to get away from God—that place is Hell.

Jonah should have known better—that even in Hell he couldn't get away from God, for even the Psalmist said, "Even if I make my bed in Hell, behold God thou art there."

The story is plain and simple. There was a storm. Cargo was thrown into the sea, Jonah slept. The sailors cast lots. The lot fell on Jonah who was cast overboard. God prepared a big fish and that fish consumed Jonah in the bowels of hell. Jonah tried everything to get out on his own. Jonah twisted! Jonah turned! Jonah squirmed! Jonah waited! Jonah hoped! But when he came to the realization that he couldn't get out of the depths of Hell on his own he cried out to the Lord and the Lord heard his cry.

Before I close this, I should tell us—*HOW TO GET OUT OF HELL.* Three ways are mentioned in this experience of Jonah.

I.   **Pray Your Way Out**

If you are in hell and you've had enough, there is a way out. First you must pray your way out. From the lips of Jonah comes these words—"*out of the belly of hell I cried and thou heardest my voice.*"

Let's back up a moment. The first step to hell is to stop talking to the Lord. The less you pray the less God can do with you. Jonah could have died in that fish's belly. But God wasn't going to let Jonah off that easy. Jonah found himself in hell and found that he couldn't get out on his own—so he prayed. Jonah would tell you, when you in hell—smarts won't get you out—contacts won't get you out— you have to pray to get out. Jonah tried everything he could—but nothing worked. Finally, Jonah prayed and the Lord heard.

If you are in hell, get on your knees and pray. Call on the Lord. God will hear. If you want out of hell you've got to pray your way out.

II. **Worship Your Way Out**

Jonah told the Lord, *"I will look again toward thy holy temple."*

Someone here—like Jonah—has stopped praying, and has thought about forsaking God's Holy Temple and making it on your own. Maybe you thought the temple was too dull and full of hypocrites. Or maybe you thought you could make it on your own without the temple. But I need to tell you nothing worked for Jonah and nothing will work for you. The temple is another way of staying in touch with God.

If you are going to find God anywhere, you will find Him in God's temple. As the prophet Habakkuk tells us—'the Lord is in His Holy Temple let all the earth keep silent before Him.' If you want to get out of hell, you have to worship your way out, praise your way out, give your way out, sing your way out, serve your way out, and shout your way out.

Worship will keep you out of hell. And worship will get you out of hell.

III. **Trust Your Way Out**

From the depths of hell, Jonah prayed to get out. He promised the Lord that once he was set free, he would go back to the temple and do everything he could do. But keep this in mind. After Jonah had done all—he simply had to wait and trust God to let him out.

Once you are in hell, you are on a when God gets ready schedule. And God may not be ready until you have learned the lesson God wants you to learn. Hell can't do anything with you without God's permission.

Jonah had done all he could do. And now he had to sit there in that hell life situation and trust and wait on God. When God decided that Jonah had suffered long enough—He spoke to that fish and it spit him out on dry land. If you trust God he will speak to whatever has a grip on your life and will set you free.

No matter how jellified the situation, if you'll pray, if you'll worship—if you'll trust—God will deliver. For salvation is of the Lord.

THREE BIG MISTAKES MANY FOLK MAKE
Scripture: James 4:13-17

"Confess your faults one to another, and pray one for another that ye may be healed. The effectual fervent prayer of a righteous man availeth much."

James 4:16

The best thing about the future is that it comes only one day at a time. Our interest should always be in the future because we are going to spend the rest of our lives there. Someone has said, and I whole-heartily agree, that "a man should never be ashamed to own that he has been in the wrong, which is but saying, in other words that he is wiser today then he was yesterday."

People make mistakes in life because we can't see ahead. If we could see the future we would do things differently. Sometimes I wish I had such a gift. If I had the gift of seeing into the future

- I would tell some young people not to marry a certain person because in ten years they are going to have three or four children, and that man will walk off and leave them for someone else.

- I could tell someone not to buy a certain car because it's a lemon and it's going to give you a lot of trouble as long as it is in your possession.

- I could tell someone not to enter that business relationship with a person because he or she will cause you to lose everything he or she now has.

Unfortunately, I do not have such a gift. No one knows what the future holds, according to the word of God. Some people seem to have the foresight to make good decisions based on the trends of the past. There are some who have the foresight to see a piece of land that no one else wants. They have the foresight to look into the future and see that particular piece of land could later be sold for millions.

There are people who have the ability to recognize talent at its early stages and turn it into something that will stagger the human mind. There are some who think they have the ability to spiritually look into the future and tell us what the future holds.

In truth, man just doesn't know what the future holds. We are able to look backward fairly clearly to our past, but we cannot look forward into the future at all. God, in His wisdom, saw fit to block the future from our minds. The Lord blocks the future from our minds because He knows it is best that we do not know what the future holds.

James deals with the future by showing us that there are *THREE BIG MISTAKES IN LIFE MANY MAKE.* I would like to share three mistakes they made during his lifetime so that we will not make the same three mistakes while we live.

I.   **The Mistakes Of Foolish Plans**

In verse 13 we read, "Go to now ye that say, today or tomorrow we will go into such a city and continue there a year, and buy and sell, and get gain."

One of the most foolish things a person can do in this life is to make plans for the future without consulting God. All of our plans should be made with the condition—*'if it is God's will.'* The Christians during James time were making foolish plans. They said, "we will go. We will buy and sell. We will stay a year." James was accusing these people of ignoring God as they made plans for the future.

There is nothing wrong with making plans for the future, but it is pure sin to leave God out of the planning process. Some people live their lives as if God did not exist. We must learn to—

- Do nothing
- Plan nothing
- Attempt to bring nothing to past, without seeking God's will in the matter.

The reason we have so many messed up lives today is because we have so many living their lives as if there is no God. We are all dangerous folk without God's controlling hand. God can do without us but we cannot do without Him. One of the three big mistakes that many make is the mistake of foolish plans.

II.   **The Mistake of Foolish Presumptions**

A presumption is a belief supported by a probability that something will happen. However it's not a sure thing—it may or may not happen.

A female student comes into a young college professor's office after hours. She kneels before him and says, pleadingly to him "I would do anything—I mean anything to pass the test you plan to give tomorrow." He returns her gaze and says, "Did you say anything?" She repeats—"Yes, I said anything." His voice turns to a whisper as he says, "Would you study?"

A lot of folk have presumed that because of what they have in terms of looks, talent and possessions; they are a jump ahead of the rest of us. But there is a mistake of foolish presumption.

Jesus told His story of the rich but foolish man who made a fortune and built up his plans for the future, and forgot that night that his soul might be required of him. How foolish it is for a man to make plans for his life, when not even tomorrow is in his control. No man has such rich friends that he can promise himself tomorrow.

It has always been the mark of a serious minded man, that he made his plans in dependence upon God. The true Christian way is not to be terrorized into fear, and not to be paralyzed into inaction by the uncertainty of the future, but to commit the future and all our plans into the hands of God and always to remember that our plans may not be within the purpose of God.

I've mentioned two big mistakes folk make—the big mistake of making foolish plans and the mistake of making foolish presumptions—and there is one more.

III. The Mistake of Foolish Postponements

Look at verse 17—James writes "Therefore to him that knoweth to do good and doth it not, to him it is sin." When we put off what we know we ought to do in the Lord's work, it is sin. There is nothing easier than not being able to find time to do those things you don't want to do. Tomorrow must be the longest day of the week judging from the number of things we are going to do then. Tomorrow may never come.

What a tragedy it would be to have to face God with unfinished business hanging over our heads. Can you imagine how it's going to be when some stand before God as Christians trying to explain all the days, weeks, months and years God gave them here on this earth and how they never got around to do what God put them here to do. Let me ask you three questions—

1. What have you been putting off in your life?
2. Have you been putting off serving the Lord?
3. Have you been putting off coming to Jesus for salvation?

Better do it today—for tomorrow may never come.

I close with this—

I stood one day at a bus stop in Cincinnati, Ohio and watched a man reach the bus stop just in time for the door to close and leave him standing there to wait another thirty minutes for the next bus to take him to his destination. In a friendly voice I said, "Sir next time you will run a little faster."

His response to me was—"Sir, I know exactly what my problem is. I ran as fast as I could. Next time I'll start sooner."

ALL MUST WORK TOGETHER OR NOTHING WORKS AT ALL
Scripture: I Corinthians 12:21-25

"And so, there are many parts, but only one body. The eye cannot say to the hand, 'I don't need you'; and the head cannot say to the foot, 'I don't need you'. Those parts of the body that we think are not worth much are the parts that we give the most care to. And we give special care to the parts of the body that we want to hide. The more beautiful parts of our body need no special care. God did this so that our body would not be divided."

The human body is absolutely amazing. One of the things that make it so amazing is how each member of our body works together with the other members to function as a healthy body. Let me introduce this message today by sharing an incident that readily explains the subject the Divine Spirit has prompted me to share with us today—"<u>All Must Work Together Or Nothing Works At All</u>".

A man once had a dream in which his hands, his feet, his mouth and his brain all began to rebel against his stomach. The hands said to his stomach, "you are really good for nothing. We work all day long sawing and hammering, lifting and carrying. By evening we're covered with blisters and scratches; our joints ache and we're covered with dirt. Meanwhile you sit there, hogging all the food."

"I agree," cried the feet. "Think how sore we get walking back and forth all day, and you just stuff yourself full like a greedy pig so that you are much heavier to carry about."

"You are so right," the mouth joined in. "Where do you think all that food you love comes from? I'm the one who has to chew it all up and as soon as I'm finished, you suck it all down for yourself. It's just not fair."

"And what about me?" called the brain. "Do you think it is easy being up here having to think about where your next meal is coming from? And yet I get nothing for all my pains."

One by one the parts of the body joined in their complaints against the stomach (also a part of the body) which didn't say a single word. "I have an idea," the brain suggested. "We get nowhere just talking about this, let's all rebel against that lazy stomach and stop working for it. We can get along just well without it. Its help is minor and insignificant. Let's quit."

So the hands stopped working. The hands refused to do any lifting and carrying; the feet refused to walk; the mouth refused to chew and swallow a single bit; and the brain swore it wouldn't come up with any more bright ideas.

At first the stomach growled a bit, as it always did when it got hungry, but after a while it was quiet. Then to the dreaming man's surprise, he found he could not walk; he could not grasp anything with his hands; he could not even open his mouth, and he suddenly began to feel ill.

The dream seemed to go on for several days. As each day passed the man felt worse. "This rebellion must not last much longer," he thought to himself—"I'll starve."

Finally the man heard a faint voice from his feet saying, "It could be that we were wrong." The feet were saying, "I suppose that stomach was working in its own way all along." "I was just thinking the same thing," said the brain. "It's true it has been getting all the food, but it seems that he has been sending most of it back to us. We might as well admit our error." The mouth said, "The stomach has just as much to do as the hands, the feet, the teeth, and the brain."

"Let's get back to work," they cried together. With that, the man woke up. To his relief he discovered his feet could walk again, his hands could grasp again, his mouth could chew again, even his brain could think clearly again.

From this dream—which could easily be termed as a nightmare—this great lesson came to him with crystal clarity—**"All Must Work Together Or Nothing Works At All"**,

Here in this scripture we find one of the most famous pictures of the unity of the church that has ever been written. Paul draws a picture of the church as a body. Now a body consists of many parts, but there is in it an essential unity. Paul draws a picture of the unity which should exist in side the church, if the church is to fulfill its proper function.

Here's something else. The body is only healthy and efficient when each part of it is functioning perfectly. The bottom line is—either we all work together or nothing works at all. Three things I'm going to say about this and I'm through.

I.   **Each Member Is Different From Every Other Member**

Let's first agree that each member of the church, as each member of the body, is different from every other member. The human body is a marvelous example of unity in diversity. There are dozens of organs performing different function, yet in such harmony there is unity.

In the church at Corinth, there had been jealousy, envy and strife among the members. Some had gifts others did not have and, as a result, they thought more highly of themselves than they should have. The result was discord and strife among the members. Paul challenged these church members to rethink and realize their relationship to one another and their relationship to Jesus Christ. He said to them—*"You are the body of Christ,"* and individually a member of it.

Each member of the church is different from every other member. Each member of the church has a place of service cut out for him or her. Under the leadership of the Spirit, it is his or her privilege and duty to discover what that place is and fill it. And, no place of service is so low as to be despised or looked down upon. No place is so high that it justifies conceit on the part of the one filling it. All must work together or nothing works at all.

II.   Each Member Devoted To The Best Interest Of Each Member

My second thought is this—each member is to be devoted to the best interest of each member. There is the suggestion of devotion to the common good. In the church selfishness is never to rule; and every man for himself is completely out of order. Paul states that since the church is a living organism, each member ought to be devoted to the highest good of every other member. When one member suffers all the members suffer with it. We are to be concerned about our brother's welfare. When one member is honored, all members are to rejoice with him or her.

Literally, we have to be the body of Christ—hands to do His work; feet to run upon His errands; and a voice to speak for Him. All must work together or nothing works at all.

III. Each Member Dependent Upon Every Other Member

My final thought is this—each member of the church is dependent upon every other member. We ought to realize that we need one another. There can be no such thing as isolation in the church.

Far too often what happens is that people in the church become so engrossed in the bit of work they are doing; so convinced of the supreme importance of the work they have given themselves that they neglect or even criticize others who have been chosen to do other work. If the church is to be a healthy body, we need the work that everyone can do. All service ranks the same with God. Work together or nothing works at all.

The late Pastor of Mt. Zion, Dr. J. H. Dotson, used to use this illustration to emphasize the unity and dedication that should exist within the church. A group of soldiers on a battlefield were standing at attention before their commissioned officer. They were told he had a dangerous and difficult assignment where he needed the help of at least ten men. There were at least fifty in the platoon.

He said, "I want volunteers. I don't want to look at you. I'm going to do an about face, and I want ten men to volunteer for this assignment. When I face you again, I want ten men to have taken ten paces forward."

The officer did as he said he was going to do. With his back turned, he heard a lot of movement, but when he faced them the formation remained the same. He began to berate them all for being cowards and willing to shirk rather than work for the winning of the battle they were in.

One team leader waited until the officer had finished his derogatory remarks and said, "Sir, you have it all wrong. We are all together in this. Not just ten men stepped forward—we all did."

The church's main purpose is to glorify God. This includes preaching God's eternal work; singing God's praises; seeking God's face in prayer; magnifying God's name in worship; fulfilling the Great Commission— telling the lost that Jesus died to save us all from our sins. "<u>**All Must Work Together Or Nothing Works At All**</u>".

CAPTER VI

*"Let your light so shine before men that they may see
your good works, and glorify your Father which is in
heaven."*

Matthew 5:16

As young George McCutchen arrived in Tulsa on that hot balmy day of
August 1953, he was not particularly thrilled with the idea of getting off
a train in a strange city, for a job interview, with no one to meet him.

Prior to the letter from Dr. Dotson about coming to Tulsa, he had
heard very little about the city. He had heard that there were many
Indians in Oklahoma, all of whom he expected to find on reservations,
and was seemingly surprised to see only a few walking the streets.

He knew that there was a renowned Evangelist-Preacher-Healer, Oral
Roberts, in Tulsa because his landlady in Nashville, Mrs. Gertrude Callier,
and his sister, Esella Zenely, were great fans of Oral Roberts.

> *"Mrs. Callier often told me of putting her hands on the radio as a
> point of contact while listening to Brother Roberts, and was healed
> from minor aches and pains. My sister longed to come to attend
> one of his Abundant Life Conferences in Tulsa."*

But, as he journeyed toward his meeting with Dr. Dotson that day,
he had good expectations for this new city in which he had come to live.
He was impressed by the number of single family dwelling places; the
number of rooming houses; and the Black owned businesses. Nashville
had many Blacks in business, but Tulsa far exceeded what he had seen.
He was impressed by the cleanliness of the city as he observed machines
sweeping and washing down the streets.

"I had lived in Cincinnati, Ohio; Louisville, Kentucky; and Nashville, Tennessee. The buildings there were black with smoke. Not so with Tulsa. Later, I was told Tulsa is one of the Nations cleanest cities—a city that bathes every night."

Dr. George Calvin McCutchen, Sr. has spent the past 54 years working in and serving the Tulsa community. It first began while he was serving as Assistant Pastor at Mt. Zion. Mr. J. A. West, a retired school teacher, and Dr. T. Harris, a pharmacist, started picking young George up to take him to the YMCA for the *"Hungary Club Luncheon Forum"*. Here he learned a lot about the community and its problems. Later he became a member of the Public Affairs Committee, and served on the Board of Management for the Hutcherson Branch YMCA.

While George was working as the Director of the North Tulsa Baptist Educational Center, he was contacted by Mrs. Jeanne Goodwin of the *"Oklahoma Eagle"*. Mrs. Goodwin felt that since he was a young minister, George would be capable of writing a column for the youth of the community. In 1956 he began writing a weekly column—**"Tips For Teens"**—for the Eagle. He wrote this column for 25 years, never missing an issue; then one day it dawned upon him that he had grown older and perhaps he was not relating well to the youth of the day, and he discontinued the column. During this time, he published two booklets on the subject that sold very well at the National Baptist Youth meetings.

George resumed his news paper writing career in 1992, when W. R. Casey, Religious Editor for the Oklahoma Eagle asked him to write a religious column for the paper. Inspired by the late Dr. J. Castina Jackson, the former pastor of Paradise Baptist Church who once wrote a column entitled "Think With Me", George decided to write **"An Invitation To Better Thinking"**. This by-weekly column had been well received by the reading public. In December 2003 the article was changed to "**Just Thinking**".

"Someone has said, only 5% of the people really think; 10% think they think; and 85% would rather die than think. In the column— "An Invitation To Better Thinking", I challenge two types of readers; those who think, and those who have stopped thinking."

George McCutchen was elected as President of the "Ministerial Alliance of North Tulsa", a position he served in for two years.

"Here I learned that ministers will put you in a position and walk off and leave you. I declined to serve as President the third year, and they elected the late Reverend B. H. Hill, who asked me to serve as his Vice-President. Because of my interest, I accepted and worked harder as Vice-President, because Reverend Hill was always absent from the meetings."

In his work with the Baptist Minister's Conference of North Tulsa, George was first elected as the Assistant Secretary, but because he made it a habit to show up on time and attended regularly, he was promoted to the Secretary's position. He worked in this position ten years, under four presidents. When the late Rev. C. R. West resigned as President, George McCutchen served as the President of this Minister's Conference for five years. He gave up this position only because he began teaching school and could not attend the weekly Monday meetings.

Later George took the position as Budget Director for the Baptist Education Center, and served there until he became President of the Oklahoma Baptist State Convention in 1990.

As Pastor of Mt. Zion Baptist Church, Dr. McCutchen was known for bring in outstanding Preacher-Evangelist from around the nation to run a week long Spring Revival each year. In 1982 Pastor McCutchen and the late Reverend H. L. Collier, Pastor of Metropolitan Baptist Church, decided that it would be beneficial to both churches to hold joint revival services. With two churches joining together the pastors felt they would be able to increase attendance and reach more people.

In 1991 Pastor T. Oscar Chappelle, Jr. and the Morning Star Baptist Church joined in on the joint revival services, and it became know as the 3M Spring Revival. The three churches were later joined by Pastor Samuel Homes and the Paradise Baptist Church, and First Baptist Church North Tulsa, to make up what is now known as the 5-Star Spring Revival.

ON DOING SOMETHING JUST TO STRETCH YOUR SOUL
Scripture: Ecclesiastes 11:1, Proverbs 11:1-25

"Cast thy bread upon the water, for thou shalt find it after many days."

Ecclesiastes 11:1

"The liberal soul shall be made fat: and he that watereth shall be watered also himself."

Proverbs 11:25

Entrance into the Kingdom depends upon one's salvation, but rewards in the Kingdom depend upon the faithful way one has served in the Lord's name. He serves God best who serves his fellowman most. When one is good to others, he is always the best to himself.

My mother told me, when I was but a small child—"Son, be good to people and somebody might just be good to you." She said—"Son, always remember that the bread comes back."

You may cast a few slices of bread on the water in an unkindly soil, in an unpromising season, but when you put it all in the hands of God; when you least expect it; your few slices of bread will come back leading a whole loaf.

The Bible says, *"Cast thy bread upon the water for thou shalt find it after many days."* The Bible also says, *"The liberal soul shall be made fat."*

I'm going to ask you to pray with me while I talk about—"<u>Doing Something To Stretch Your Soul</u>". Let me explain the subject of this message by sharing an experience that was mine with a man who owned an operated a shoe repair business in our community.

One day I left a pair of badly worn shoes with Mr. E. L. Madison, Sr. to be repaired. I returned on the promised day to pick them up with only $20.00 in my pocket. The man gave me the shoes looking almost like new. I attempted to give him the twenty dollar bill, expecting him to ask for more. Had he asked for more, I would have told him I would get them the next week, but to my utter amazement he told me to put my money back in my pocket.

Not used to being on the receiving end, I demanded from him an explanation. The devil gave me the thought that since my shoes were so badly worn, that maybe he felt I was just too poor to pay. I then demanded that I be allowed to give him something for a job so well done.

What made me understand him and walk away satisfied was two things he said which I will never forget. First he said, "It takes as much grace to receive a gift as it does to give one." Secondly he said, "A Christian ought to do something every now and then just to stretch his soul."

Therefore, I'm going to ask you to pull up a chair and listen as I talk about <u>Doing Something To Stretch Your Soul</u>.

I.   **We Live In A Selfish Materialistic World**

First, I call our attention to the fact that this is a selfish, materialistic world in which we live. When it comes to this matter of casting bread upon the water and doing some soul stretching, one question many ask is—What's in it for me.

Some folk will cast a piece of stale bread upon the water and expect chocolate cake in return. Not many, if any, think much about doing something just to stretch their souls. Their philosophy of life is not to earn all you can, save all you can, and give all you can. Their philosophy of life is to get all you can, to can all you get, then sit on the can. Because of this their souls are becoming shriveled up, and it is all because of their self-centeredness and greed.

I've stopped by here tonight, on my way to Heaven, to tell somebody that a Christian ought to do something every now and then just to stretch their soul.

II.   **Some Souls Need A Lot Of Stretching**

Speaking on doing something to stretch your soul, you must agree with me that there are some folk you and I know whose souls could stand a whole lot of stretching.

Out of my bag of memories, the occasional visits of my Uncle George arise. I often wonder why my parents named me after him.

The man made the wrong impressions on me. I remember him for his love of money.

He was my mother's brother, and my father said that he was as tight as dried eggs on a plate and he could squeeze a dollar until '*Ole George*' on it turned blue.

One day Uncle George was handling his money and dropped a penny. His eyesight was dim, so I found it for him. Holding it out to him, I childishly thought he would give it to me. Instead, he snatched it out of my hand and said—"Thank you child. I knew those young eyes of yours would find it for me." Into that snap top leather pocketbook it went, to keep company with all of his other coins.

Just think—for one penny I would have remembered him as being a very generous man instead of the stingy fellow he was. Only in recent years did I figure out why he didn't give me that penny. He loved his money more than he loved me.

The sad thing about it, when he died, he didn't take a dime with him. Had he shared with his little snotty nosed, barefooted nephew, it might have been like sending some of it on before. There are some folk all of us know whose souls could stand a little stretching.

III. **Soul Stretching Keeps Our Priorities In Proper Perspective**

Another reason folk ought to do some soul stretching—such, helps us as Christians to keep our priorities in the proper perspective. The Master said, "*Seek ye first the Kingdom of God and His righteousness, then all other things you need will be given to you.*"

Most of us are slow to believe it, but the better things in life are those things that money can't buy. For instance money can buy a beauty rest inner-spring mattress, but it will not buy one wink of sleep. Even a thematically controlled water bed will not ease a troubled mind. With money you can buy the choicest food, but it will not buy an appetite. With money you can take a dream vacation to the exotic corners of the world, but it will not take you away from yourself.

Folk need to stretch their souls—such, helps Christians to keep their priorities in the proper perspective.

IV. **Soul Stretching Stands Firmly On The Promises Of God**

Finally, I think I need to tell us that with a stretched soul, one stands more firmly on the promises of God.

There is nothing like a Christian. They prefer to believe, and believe without a doubt, without a question, and without delay that God has said what He meant and meant what He said, and has rearranged their personal lives accordingly.

I hear folk say—"I'm not going to allow anyone to use me". But, Christians believe that Jesus is good for whatever is bad, and right for whatever is wrong. The Christian believes what Paul said—"*Be not weary in well doing, in due season we will reap the harvest if we faint not.*"

Be ye steadfast, unmovable, and always abounding in the work of the Lord. With a stretched soul, the Christian stand more firmly on the promises of God.

I'd like to close this message with the story often told of a Missionary who had given many years of his life on a foreign field. Because of failing health and his inability to cope with the problems of his work, he was sent a ticket by his mission board to come back to the States and retire. He came from Africa, and happened to be on the same plane with Theodore Roosevelt who had been there on a hunting safari.

When the President arrived in New Your, there was a great crowd to welcome him. He was given VIP treatment all the way.

When the Missionary got off the plane, no one from his board met him. He was forced to carry his own luggage and find his way to a cheap hotel for the night. When in his room that night he and the Lord did some heart to heart talking. He told the Lord—"Life just isn't fair. Life has issued me a lemon. I've given my best and have received the worse. The President, who has given least in your service, receives the best. He comes home and is showered with everything and I come home with nothing."

When he got up from his prayer, he says the lord talked to him. The Lord told him—"Give me more time. I'm going to make it up to you. You haven't come home yet."

He who does God's work will receive God's pay. On our regular time clocks, sometimes the clock is inaccurate; our check comes out too much or too little. But, God's time clock is well regulated. He knows how much work we have done. He's going to pay me for all I have done.

> ## HOW NOT TO GET TIRED OF TRYING TO DO GOOD
> Scripture: Galatians 6:9-10

"And let us not grow weary while doing good, for in due season we shall reap, if we do not lose heart. Therefore as we have opportunity, let us do good to all, especially to those who are of the household of faith."

(NKJV) Galatians 6:9-10

Let me introduce this message today with an article I read many years ago in The Saturday Evening Post. It is an article written by a young man—who refused to give his name. His subject was—"*Why I Quit The Gospel Ministry.*" He was a young man who—the Lord had blessed to serve several of the nation's most prominent churches. Even so, in this article he told quite frankly the painful story of why he quit. He cited several reasons in an effort to justify his actions.

First, he complained that the membership for the most part didn't want to hear Christ's ideas of Christianity. He cited that a little clique ran the church. He said the churches he had served were divided into two groups—those who ran the church and those who spent their time trying to block the runners.

He went on to say that of a membership of 800 on the rolls—only about half were regular in attendance and consistent in their financial support. And to add to that—he was of the opinion that only a small minority (if any) put the church first in their lives. He further stated that the churches God had permitted him to serve—the members acted as though they weren't interested in developing spiritually.

His Sunday School teachers and Ministry leaders didn't want to improve the educational program of the church. For those who were placed in positions of leadership were (in his own words) like an old mule he remembered while growing up on his father's farm. They were backward in the art of moving forward.

He continued to say that he observed that (and this was the hardest part) from all of his hard labor, day and night, to the extent of nine days a week, he could see so little in terms of results. With all of his preaching, his praying, shouting and singing, the world seemed to go unchanged unless it was getting worse. He closed the article by clearly stating—I quit the Gospel Ministry because <u>I Got Tired of Trying to do Good.</u>

When I read that article, which was several years ago, I began to look at my own ministry. I did some looking back at the road over which I have traveled—"I've had some good days, I've had some bad days. I've had some dreary days, and some sleepless nights—but when I look around and I think things over—etc. I'm fully aware of this fact—Like the Apostle Paul, I was made a Minister and the Gospel Ministry has been my very life. Take me out of the Ministry would be like taking a fish out of a flowing stream.

During the almost 46 years I've been trying to serve the Lord—I'm too blessed to complain. I have always been conscientious of having a loyal congregation who loved me enough to mention my name to the Lord in their prayers. For the most part—most people—are kind, generous, gracious and sympathetic. Without God's help—no preacher would be equaled to the task.

I would report to you today, in spite of all I've been through—my disappointments, my frustrations, and my up and down experiences—I have been content to go on with the Lord. And I've stopped by here this afternoon on my way to Heaven, to tell another one of my sons in the Gospel Ministry—How Not to Get Tired of Trying to do Good.

In the language of our text, Paul writes—"*And let us not grow weary, while doing good, for in due season, we shall reap if we do not lose heart.*

Therefore as we have opportunity, let us do good to all men especially to those who are of the household of faith."

Pray with me while I talk from the all important subject—"**How to Keep from Getting Tired of Trying to do Good**." I shall mention a few thoughts the Divine Spirit has shared with me—and I'm through.

I.   **Be A Responsible Self-Manager**

One way Not to Get Tired of Trying to do Good is by being a responsible self-manager. I've known executives who were experts in managing the affairs of the company they work for who could not manage their own lives.

Travel the road to self-management—the results will far outweigh the effort. The Bible says, *"He that ruleth his spirit is better than he that taketh a city."* (Proverbs 16:32)

We have an "ugly self" and a "saintly self." One is as bad as the other—unless it's controlled by the Divine Spirit. Paul speaks of self-management—when he said, *"The good I would I do not, and the evil I would not that I do. I have to beat my body to bring it under subjection, else aptly after I have preached to others, I myself may be a cast away."*

To keep from getting tired of tying to do good one has to shift gears from ego to the altar, from self to others, from self centeredness to Christ centeredness. We need to teach ourselves—if you can't get what you want—want what you get. To keep from getting tired of trying to do good—be a responsible manager of yourself.

II. **Do It By The Day**

Secondly, To Keep From Getting Tired of Trying to Do Good—try doing it by the day. When you wake up in the morning—be careful to say to yourself—"This is a day the Lord has made. I will rejoice and be glad in it." Tell the Lord—"nothing is going to come up this day that you and I can't work out together." Do it by the day. Today is all you have—today is all you need—today is all you can manage.

Someone asked a giant oak tree—how did you come to be as stately as you are? Its reply was, "By growing a little wood every day." To keep from Getting Tired of Trying to Do Good—Try it by the day.

III. **Stay Close To Jesus Christ—Never Give Up Your Faith**

Finally, I would suggest to Keep From Getting Tired of Trying to Do Good—one must stay close to Jesus Christ and never give up your faith in God. Christ is the believer's strength. Paul said, *"I can do all things through Christ which strengtheth me. In Him we live and move and have our being."*

To keep from Getting Tired of Trying to do Good—you will have to "lean on His everlasting arm." Live close to Christ—say with the songwriter—*"Thou my everlasting portion, more than friend or life to me, All along this pilgrim journey, Savior, let me walk with Thee. Not for ease or worldly pleasures, nor for fame—my prayer shall be, Gladly will I toil and suffer, only let me walk with Thee.*

Stay plugged into the power—stay close to Jesus Christ. Never give up your faith in God for without God—You will find yourself falling beneath the load; you will find yourself fighting a losing battle; you will find yourself biting off more than you can chew. Without God you will find yourself committing your soul to a godless and miserable eternity.

Without Him little things will irritate you to no end; daily routines will become nothing but a rat race; and without God you will find yourself miserable even in the midst of those who love you.

God can lift your heavy burdens no matter how heavy they might be. God can calm your nerves no matter how tense they may be. God can change your circumstances no matter how pathetic they may be.

- God can turn burdens into blessings.
- God can turn weakness into strength.
- God can turn fear into faith.
- He has an arm safe enough to lean on.
- He can guide your faltering footsteps.
- He can catch you when you're falling.

- He can bring you back should you go astray.

Don't ever give up your Faith in God.

IT COST TO BE THE BOSS
Scripture: Mark 10:35-37; Luke 12:48a

"And James and John, the sons of Zebedee, come unto Him, saying, "Master we would that thou shouldest do for us whatsoever we shall desire." And he said unto them "What would ye, that I should do for you." They said unto Him, grant unto us that we may sit, one on the right hand, and the other on the left hand in thy glory."

Mark 10:35-37

"For unto whomsoever much is given, of him shall be much required."

Luke 12:48a

The human mind has the amazing ability for rejecting that which it does not wish to contain, just as the human ear has the amazing capacity for tuning out that which it does not wish to hear. Because of this, folk still accept the parts of the Christian message which they like and they refuse to understand anything that is foreign to their way of thinking.

Our Lord's ministry was not only to people in general. He was often forced to minister to people individually. Sometimes, He was forced to minister to His disciples—His chosen and closest friends. In these scriptures the divine spirit has given me to talk from today—the Master gives to each of us a principle it would do well for us to keep and practice (at least remember) throughout all the days of our lives.

We don't like to talk about it too much, but the Master taught that more is expected of some than of others. If a man or woman is more fully honored than another—folk have a right to expect more of him or her. My subject today is "<u>It Cost To Be The Boss</u>." In Luke the 12th Chapter and a portion of that 48th verse—Jesus said *"For unto whomsoever much is given much of him shall be much required."* Let me explain this subject by sharing an experience that was mine just a few years ago. I had finished a series of lectures at a church in a distant city. On Saturday, the custom is—the Pastor and his Deacons take their church van and together they go out to breakfast. This is not a Dutch treat, they alternate picking up the tab for the meal.

Since I, as well as another minister were their guests, and it was not yet time for us to depart from their city, we were invited to be a part of their fellowship. Since it is nice to be nice and when they are nice they don't have to be nice to you—we wholeheartedly accepted their kind invitation. As we rode along together, these fellows with their Pastor, entered into a discussion as to whose time it was to pay. The Chairman of their Board must have given the other fellows that impression that he was a little tight-fisted in departing from his personal funds. They told him—"It's your turn, your time to pay." His question was—"Of all days, we have two extra folk here and I can look at these fellows. They aren't accustomed to eating a continental breakfast. Why must I pay today?" One fellow's response was this "You're the Boss and it costs to be the Boss."

There are three things I wish to say and I'm through.

1. First I want to call our attention to the fact that folk often seek high places with low motives.
2. The greater the privilege—the greater the responsibility.
3. One's ambition must never be substituted for a desire to serve; for the higher one rises the larger their service should be.

Pray with me while I talk from this all important subject—"<u>**It Cost To Be The Boss**</u>".

I.   **Folk Seek High Places With Low Motives**

Mark tells an experience in the life of the Master. They were on their way to Jerusalem. Many who followed Him were afraid for Him to go. Therefore He took His 12 aside and shared with them all that would happen to Him while there. He would be tried, convicted, condemned. He would also be beaten and nailed to a cross. But He would die and rise again after three days.

The record shows that James and John thought that since victory will be Yours and the triumph will be complete, we want a share of Your glory. The Bible says, "They came to Jesus and said, 'Teacher we want You to do for us whatever we ask." Jesus quickly responded, 'What do you want me to do for you?' Let one of us sit at your right hand and the other at the left when You come into Your glory."

Some of the authorities have agreed that they sought high places—with low motives. They appeared to be more into sitting than in serving. They wanted the glory without the gory. They wanted gains without pains; the crown without bearing the cross. Jesus was careful to tell them—"It Costs to be the Boss." The places belonged to those for whom they had been prepared.

I need not remind us that the situation today has not changed. Many today desire to serve only in an advisory capacity. Somebody needs to tell us—to evade the cross is to forfeit being the boss. Folk seek high places with low motives.

This brings me to the next thought.

II. **One's Ambition To Rule Must Never Take The Place Of One's Desire To Serve**

Jesus, knowing human nature as He did, didn't condemn human ambition. He didn't condemn His followers for being ambitious. But He was careful to remind them that their ambition to rule must not be allowed to supersede their desire to serve. It costs to be the Boss.

Jesus was careful to point out to these disciples two important facts

- The title "Boss" in the Kingdom enterprise is reserved for the one who is willing to do the most in it.
- And it is not "Kings" but servants who get to be the boss in the Lord's Kingdom.

One's desire to rule must never take the place of the ambition to serve.

III. **The Higher One Rises The Greater The Servant One Must Be**

The final thought is this—the higher one rises in the eyes of people and in the sight of God, the greater the servant one must be.

It is a principle in Scripture that one must start as a servant before he becomes a ruler, if he ever expects to be one. This explains why David was such a success as a King. He began as a servant, a humble shepherd boy. He proved that he could be trusted, that he could get the job done.

The person who lacks the knowledge of what it means to be under authority has no right to exercise authority over others. One's faithfulness in little things determines one's readiness for being responsible for larger matters.

Before closing, a few principles the "Boss" must remember. First, the "Boss" can't expect anyone to do more than he or she is willing to do themselves. The idea of not doing as I do but as I say won't work. The Boss is expected to be a good example to those who come under His command. Another thing—we need to remember the Boss can't be a beggar too.

This as I close—be determined to find out your strengths so that you can give them in service.

A man tells of browsing through a gift shop near Ashville, North Carolina. He was fascinated by the number of wood-carvings that were on display. Picking up a carved "hound dog" he asked, "How in the world does someone go about carving a wooden hound dog?"

"Well first" the man said, "I take a piece of wood this size, then I take out my pocket knife and I whittle away all the extra wood that don't look like no hound dog."

There is a message here—carve and whittle away all those things, especially those extra things that would keep you from using your special gift for God in His service. Carve away at those areas in your life that would impede your work for the Lord. Discover your unusual abilities— then use them in God's service.

DON'T PUT OUT THE FIRE
Scripture Leviticus 6:13; I Thessalonians 5:19

"A fire shall always be burning on the altar; it shall never go out."

Leviticus 6:13

"Do not quench the Spirit."

I Thessalonians 5:19

Among the Hebrew people in ancient times, fire was the manifestation of the very presence of God. Our heart-fixing and mind regulating God has made His presence known to His people by fire. The record shows that God made His presence known to Moses by fire. He spoke to Moses from a burning bush on the back-side of a mountain. That bush in a desert place was burning and it was not consumed. That burning bush was a fine representation of an eternal and ever-lasting God.

God led Israel through the wilderness with a pillar of fire. That fire served as a lamp by night and a cloud by day.

God assured His prophet Elijah that his prayers had been heard on Mount Carmel Elijah won a great victory over 450 prophets of Baal, because God manifested His presence on water soaked altar in a little flame of fire. Fire was first used on the altar by Noah when they came from the ark.

Our text today reminds us that fire was used in connection with the sacred worship under the Levitical priesthood. It was the duty of the priests to keep the fire burning. The fire was to ever be burning on the altar of sacrifice. The Bible says, "It was never to go out." Every evening a lamb would be sacrificed. It would be placed on the altar. It was to remain there all night until the morning. The priest would remove from the altar the ashes the fire had left. Then place fresh wood on the fire. The altar fire was never to go out.

- The ever burning fire on the altar symbolized Israel's unceasing worship of God.
- The ever burning fire also symbolized God's unceasing acceptance of Israel as His chosen people.
- The priest was charged with the responsibility to keep the fire burning.
- Two things the priest were to do—ONE—he had to lay on the altar more wood; TWO—he had to keep the ashes removed. This required some labor on the part of the priest.

God had said to His people "The fire shall always be burning on the altar. It shall never go out."

Pray with me while I talk from this all important subject—"**DON'T PUT OUT THE FIRE**". Three things I'm going to say about this and I'm through.

I.   **The Presence Of The Holy Spirit in the Church Today**

First of all, the fire on the altar in ancient times symbolized the presence of the Holy Spirit in the church today.

After our Lord's death, burial and resurrection—before He ascended into Heaven to be at the right hand of the Father—He told a group of believers to go to Jerusalem—to tarry there—and wait for the fire. The record shows that while 120 believers waited and prayed there in the upper room—the day of Pentecost fully came. The Bible says, "There appeared to them divided tongues, as of fire, and one sat upon each one of them." The Holy Spirit came as a burning fire. That fire started burning on the altar of their hearts and they couldn't hold their peace.

The Day of Pentecost has been referred to as the birthday of the Church. When the fire begins to burn, it is a visible sign that the church's doors are open for business. And the fire is to never go out. As a matter of act, if the fire should go out—church is over.

The Spirit of God acts upon a believer's nature like a fire. Fire warms, it purifies and it revives—we need the fire. The fire of the Holy Spirit is not to be quenched. Christ came to Baptize with the Holy Spirit. The Holy Spirit came also to baptize with fire. Don't put out the fire. He who has felt the fire—should never fight the feeling. Paul admonishes the believers at Thessalonica, *"Quench not the Spirit; don't put out the fire."*

II.   **The Church Needs The Fire—We Need The Fire**

Secondly, we must not put out the fire because the church needs the fire. We need the fire. There is no clear revelation from Heaven without the fire. Heaven would be as black as midnight and as dry as a grave without the fire. God cannot be glorified; souls cannot be edified; souls cannot be saved, and backsliders cannot be reclaimed, without the fire. We need the fire.

In the Old Testament the priest had to do it all to keep the fire burning. In the Old Testament, the Priest had to remove the ashes and add wood to the flame. But now, since Jesus came, every believer is his or her own priest. Every believer is charged with the responsibility of laying on wood and removing the ashes. You got to keep the fire burning.

Some folk have become indifferent towards the church. Don't blame the church. Some folk have gotten cold. Don't blame the church. You are responsible. You have to keep your own fire burning. You might need to move closer to the fire. Some folk are too far from the fire.

- The fire is in the Sunday School.
- The fire is in the Prayer Service.
- The fire is in the Bible Study.
- The fire is in a Spiritual Sermon.

Some folk are too far from the fire.

You say the fire is not the same. Remove the ashes on your altar. I refer to

- The ashes of doubt
- The ashes of jealousy
- The ashes of envy
- The ashes of unforgiveness and
- The ashes of grudges

We need the fire—Don't put out the fire.

III. **The Fire Has To Be Stirred Up**

The third and last thing I want to tell you is the fire you got has to be stirred up. Fire that just sits and sits without any stirring will soon burn out.

During my preaching career of the past 50 years—I have preached in many places in this nation, and in other countries of this world. Pastors have told me of the many needs their churches have. The needs vary from kitchen facilities, class-rooms, to parking spaces.

Some claim they need more members. The finances are low so they say—we need more money—better leaders—more youth—a radio or television ministry. But what we need most is the fire of God's spirit. Jesus said, *"And I if I be lifted up from the earth...."*

Satan is always busy sowing discord, disharmony and confusion among the members. He's trying to put out our fire. Satan has a fire department going from church to church putting out fires. If you are not careful Satan will put out your fire.

Jeremiah almost made this terrible mistake. Jeremiah was terribly discouraged, preaching to folk who would not listen to all he had to say. But every time he tried to quit, the word of God, he said, was like a burning fire shut up in his bones and he couldn't hold his peace.

The devil has organizers in the church whose sole business is to put out the fire in the church. To combat the devil's organizers— God needs more agonizers.

- Prayer kindles the fire.
- Prayer chunks up the fire.
- Prayer keeps the fire burning.

Our job as believers is to keep the fire stirred up. Keep the fire burning. It's our responsibility to keep the fires burning.

WHEN YOU REACH THE BOTTOM OF THE BARREL
Scripture: I Kings 17:10-12

"So he arose and went to Zarephath. And when he came to the gate of the city, indeed a widow was there gathering sticks. And he called to her and said, "Please bring me a little water, in a cup that I might drink." And as she was going to get it, he called to her and said, "Please bring me a morsel of bread in your hand."

So she said, "As the Lord your God lives, I do not have bread, only a handful of flour in a bin, and a little oil in a jar, and see

*I am gathering a couple of sticks that I might go in and prepare
it for myself and my son, that we might eat it and die."*

I Kings 17:10-12 (NKJV)

In these few verses I've read in your hearing, we are given a classic
example of what can happen when we release the limb of our security and
put our trust completely in God. Our text is lifted from the story of a
widow whose name we do not know. The Bible simple refers to her as the
widow of Zarephath. In her story we find a miracle of trust.

During the time this incident occurred, her land was experiencing a
great drought. It hadn't rained for months. The rivers were drying up—
all crops in the fields were failing. Because of the lack of food, many were
dying of starvation and this widow and her small son were no exception.

On this particular day, she found herself with only a little meal left in
her barrel and a small corner of cooking oil in her cruse—just enough for
one last meal for herself and her son.

She had resigned herself to the fact that when this was gone she and
her son would die. What a terrible fate. What a horrible ending—the
idea of starving to death. This would seem to be the end of her story—
but in fact it was only the beginning. God had a different plan. God
had visited this scene before this widow's problem ever came to be. And
I'm going to ask you to pull up a chair and listen while I talk from this
subject—"<u>When You Reach The Bottom Of The Barrel</u>".

There are at least four things one needs to know.

I.   **When Need Is Greatest—God Is Nearest**

First, can I tell you when your need is the greatest, God is the
nearest. I'm a witness to this in my own experiences. We will never
have a problem that takes God by surprise. Whether it be a mountain
of impossibility or a valley of despair—God has already surveyed it
and is waiting to guide you and I through it.

As the great Master Planner, He has already chosen the paths
before us. He knows not his own strength who has not met
adversity. Heaven prepares good folk with the crosses they are forced
to carry. When we find that we are up against it—it's because we

back up instead of going ahead. When you reach the bottom of your barrel—remember this spiritual truth—when our need is the greatest God is the nearest.

II.   Our Last Supply Becomes God's First Concern

My second thought is this—our last supply becomes god's first concern. Humanly speaking, the widow of Zarephath had reached the bottom of her barrel when the prophet of God told her to bring him a little morsel of bread and with that a cup of water. She had to admit that she didn't have a cake only a handful of meal in a barrel and a little oil in a cruse. Yet the prophet told her—God told me that I would be sustained by you. Your last supply is God's first concern—so fix me some bread first.

She had reached the end of her earthly supply. She had no one but God to save her. Her human resources were depleted and trusting was her only hope. And what hope she found.

His love has no limits.

His grace has no measure

His power has no boundary known unto man.

For out of His infinite riches in Jesus, He giveth and giveth and giveth again.

When we reach the end of our self sufficiency and find ourselves at the bottom of the barrel of life—we too can have the reassurance that God is still there. He is lovingly and tenderly reaching out to us to meet us at the point of our greatest need. When all else has failed we can always depend on Him. Our last supply becomes God's first concern.

III.   God Asks Much When He Wants To Give Much

Another thought comes to mind—when you have reached the bottom of the barrel, God asks much when He wants to give much. When this widow told the prophet Elijah of her plight, he did the very opposite of what most of us would have expected him to do. Instead of revealing to her that he was sent by God to meet her needs, he told her to make something for himself first and feed herself and her son with the leftovers. It appears that the prophet was insensitive and selfish. He asked for the greatest possession in this widow's life. It was like asking for her life itself.

Let me tell us here—God asks the same of us today—total surrender to Him the greatest possession of our lives. But He is not trying to rob us of our joy. He's not trying to take away from us those things that make us happy. He's just trying to teach us a lesson. He wants us to want nothing in our lives to be greater than He is. Nothing we trust more than we trust Him.

When this widow gave all she had she was acknowledging that God had first priority in her life.

Can I tell you—the more we trust God with the details of our lives, the more we will see His blessings in our lives. God asks much when He wants to give much.

This brings me to my final thought.

IV. **God Blesses in Abundance**

I already said—when our need is greatest, God is nearest; Our last supply is His first concern; God asks much when He wants to give much. Can I now tell us—when we give in faith, God blesses in abundance.

This story of Elijah and the widow has a very beautiful ending. Once she fed the prophet by faith, and put her confidence in God, the scripture says, *"And her barrel of meal wasted not, and neither did her cruse of oil fail, according to the words of the Lord, as He spoke unto Elijah."*

Note God not only kept His promise, He did it in abundance. He met every need the widow and her son had. The Bible says as long as the famine was in the land, her meal barrel was never empty and her cruse of oil never failed. We may not always be able to determine how God will answer our prayers and meet our needs.

The story is often told of a woman who prayed for two sacks of flour. Two mischievous boys, who were known in the neighborhood, were playing nearby and heard her praying. The boys went to the grocery, bought two sacks of flour and left them for the woman to find. When she said thank you for answering my prayer—the boys said to her, "God ain't done no such thing. We brought you them sacks of flour."

The woman turned to these boys and said, "Boys, God did send the flour to me, even if He had to use two little devils to bring it."

Just as this widow of Zarephath trusted God when she reached the bottom of her barrel, so must you and I learn the miracle of trust in our own lives. God works in our hearts to produce this miracle of trust. God wants us to know that He is always there—and His power is always at work on our behalf. We never have to face any of our pressures and problems alone. An all wise and all loving God will always provide exactly what we need when we need it.

He who gives to me teaches me to give. A rejected opportunity to give is a lost opportunity to receive.

CHAPTER VII

"For everyone who exalts himself will be humbled, and
he who humbles himself will be exalted."

Luke 14:11

The early Sixties was a changing time for the Tulsa Public School System. Although the pupils had not integrated the schools, the teachers were being integrated into the system.

In a conversation with his friend, A. L. Morgan of Marion Anderson Junior High School, young George McCutchen learned of problems with this integration. Mr. Morgan remarked that the new teacher's dedication was not as great as teachers of the past. Someone was always out for one reason or another.

> *"I told my friend that I was a college graduate. I majored in History, and had a minor in English and Social Studies. Maybe I could help."*

At Mr. Morgan's suggestion, young George went to the Educational Service Center and applied to be a *Substitute Teacher*. Before the final approval of the School Board was received, George McCutchen was called to work almost every day at one of the area schools. He worked for two years with a temporary certificate, substituting at Roosevelt, Cleveland, Carver, Hamilton, and Monroe Junior High Schools, and McLain Senior High. The pay at that time was $23.00 a day, which was a blessed addition to his salary at Mt. Zion.

> *"I enjoyed being in the classroom. Teaching kids was a great challenge. Mr. Greadington, Principal at Marion Anderson Middle School, asked me one day how I managed to keep the children quiet and orderly. My reply was—I'm bigger than they are."*

The day soon arrived when the young people began to show little respect for authority. Fearful that he might get into trouble with his old fashioned methods of discipline, George decided to bring his teaching career to a halt.

The Sixties were also not stress free years for the City of Tulsa, for just like other cities across the United States, Tulsa was in the middle of the Civil Rights Movement. These were the years when Black protest brought down years of segregation.

> *"I have lived in Tulsa more than 54 years. Tulsa, as a city, has gone through a lot of changes. Race relations have changed, but not too much. There are no longer segregated public accommodations, but there are plenty of reminders that there is a difference."*

George McCutchen saw the need and the importance of such a movement, and joined with Reverend B. S. Roberts in the Christian Education Protest Movement. He met weekly with youth groups, training them for staging sit-ins to challenge segregation in public places.

They went to different places to test whether they would be served. They spent a lot of personal money, because sometimes establishments would serve them and the tab for the fifty to sixty students would have to be paid. But many times establishments would not serve the group and, if they refused to leave, they would be jailed.

Adelene McCutchen, who had worked as a registered nurse at Morton Hospital for the past ten years, decided she needed a career change. She wanted a *"less stressful"* job, so she decided to become Tulsa's Second Black Policewoman.

> *"My wife chose the wrong time for her career change, because I was in charge of some of the youth groups that she had to arrest."*

Adelene worked twenty years for the Tulsa Police Department, fifteen years as a juvenile officer and five years handling sex offender cases.

Out of respect for Adelene's position, and because they could not run the risk of her losing her job, Reverend Roberts insisted that George would leave the establishments when asked to do so, in order to avoid being arrested.

> *"I've lived in North Tulsa for the past 54 years. I am impressed that if I had the means to do so I could live anywhere in the city or in the suburbia of Broken Arrow, Glenpool, Jenks, or Owasso. I like Tulsa; and the chances are I will remain in Tulsa after I retire from active pasturing. I used to ask my family to take me to the Hills of Kentucky to be buried. But I've decided that here I have served, and here will be my final resting place."*

In 2002 Pastor McCutchen and several other pastors and leaders in the North Tulsa Community saw the need to reach out to help control the violence and disturbances in the area. These leaders started a movement where they would walk the streets after the clubs closed at 2:00 a.m. to try to turn the young people around.

Knowing that he does not have the inability to say "NO" when asked to serve, it is safe to say that Pastor McCutchen has preached at most of the churches in the Tulsa community and surrounding areas. He has led revival meetings, taught study courses, and just been a participant on programs when needed and asked.

A Charter Member of the Tulsa North SERTOMA Club, Dr. McCutchen has served as a board member for the Youth Services, Inc.; Metropolitan Tulsa Urban League; One Church—One Child, Inc.; and the Martin Luther King Commemoration Committee. He has served as past President of the T. Oscar Chappelle, Sr., Oklahoma School of Religion; Program Chairman and Sunday School Teacher for the Baptist Ministers Conference of North Tulsa; Vice-President of Tulsa Together; and is a member of Pyramid Lodge #69 and the Tulsa Ten Point Coalition.

Fifty-four years ago George Calvin McCutchen, a young man just out of Seminary School, *One Of The Whosoevers* stopped by the Tulsa Community. He made his mark on Tulsa and the surrounding areas, and has received numerous awards and recognitions for his work including the—

- Zeta Phi Beta Sorority Community Service Award (1983)

- Benjamin Franklin Service Award—Southeast Tulsa SERTOMA (1988)
- Baptist Minister's Conference Service Award (1990)
- Tulsa Branch NAACP Freedom Through Education Award (1993)
- Greenwood Image Builders Award from the North Tulsa Heritage Foundation (1996)
- Outstanding Service Award—Christian Minister's Conference (1996)
- Recognition for years of Outstanding Contributions to Interfaith Understanding from the Jewish Federation of National Conference, Tulsa Metropolitan Ministry.

Dr. George Calvin McCutchen, Sr. continues to make his mark on the community as he continues to share his belief, his goals, and his experience with others.

I'VE NEVER BEEN DISAPPOINTED IN JESUS
Scripture: Psalm 37:25; psalm 34:8

"I have been young and now I'm old—yet I have not seen the righteous forsaken, nor His seed seeking bread."

Psalm 37:35

"Oh taste and see that the Lord is good; blessed is the man that trusteth in Him."

Psalm 34:8

There has never been a soul who has not time and time again tasted of the drags of disappointment. Disappointment seemingly can arise from almost any service. There have been times—

- When Congressmen and even Presidents have disappointed us;
- When advisors have disappointed us;
- When investments have disappointed us;
- When repairmen of appliances, even of automobiles have disappointed us.

There has never been a soul, and there perhaps never will be a soul, who has not time and again tasted of the bitter dregs of disappointment.

Regardless of who you are; where you were raised or where you have been; what your circumstances are or have been; there have been times in your life when you were disappointed.

I have been told about parents who were disappointed by their children. I have been told of children that were disappointed with their parents. I have been told of different times when doctors have disappointed their patients; when lawyers have disappointed their clients; when bankers have disappointed their depositors; when teachers have disappointed their students and students have disappointed their teachers; when automobiles have disappointed their owners.

But, I beg to submit to us today that Jesus has never, never disappointed you or anybody else who placed their faith and trust in Him; who looked to Him as their savior and redeemer. Nobody, myself included, has never been disappointed in Jesus.

There are four things I'm going to ask you to pray with me while I share, and I'm through.

1. First I want to call our attention to the fact that we have all experienced great and painful disappointments in people, places, and things.

2. Secondly I want us to agree that we have all sometimes been a disappointment to ourselves.

3. Then I want us to confess that we have at some time, some where, sadly disappointed the Lord.

4. Finally, I'm going to ask you to agree and say with me—I've never been disappointed in Jesus.

I.   **Disappointments In People, Places, and Things**

We have all experienced great and painful disappointments in people. There have been a few times when I became disappointed in a Sunday School teacher, church officer, special singer, musician, evangelist or preacher, but I have never been disappointed with Jesus. I've been disappointed with people.

I've been disappointed with places I have been; disappointed with trips and vacations. I have gone to places which were termed as places of enjoyment, and left there disappointed.

I've been disappointed in things. I've been disappointed with books I've read; with insurance policies; even with cars I have purchased.

We are all human, and we all have our share of faults and failures; therefore, I can understand and accept all of the disappointments I have had. But, one thing I know for sure—I've never been disappointed in Jesus.

II.   A Disappointment To Ourselves

I'm sure we have been a disappointment to ourselves. I don't know about you—I can only speak for myself—but I can tell you this morning that there have been many times in my life when I felt I could have done better than I did. When I could have helped more; prayed longer; studied harder; loved deeper; given more than I did.

I've disappointed myself so many times, but I've never been disappointed with my Lord and Savior, Jesus Christ.

III. A Disappointment To Him

I've disappointed and I've been a disappointment to Him. If you are as honest as you should be, you will join me in admitting that we have sadly disappointed the Lord. For example—

- When we said what we should not have said;
- When we went where we should not have gone;
- When we did what we should not have done;
- When we thought what we should not have thought
- When we desired what we should not have desired; even assumed what we should not have assumed.

Yes, I am sure that the Lord has been disappointed in me and you. But let me tell you one more time—nobody has ever been disappointed in Jesus.

Let me move quickly into my final, but most important point of this message today.

IV.   I Am Not Disappointed With My Lord

I am not disappointed in how the Lord operates His business. I am not disappointed in how He reveals it. I am not disappointed in how He paints the sunrise or the sunset; in how He causes the flowers to bloom and emit their fragrance; in how He sustains this vast universe—this vast creation.

I am not disappointed in how He planned the universe; how He made the sun to shine;; how He gave the moon its glow; how He carved out the mountains; how He set limit on the ocean; in how He taught the birds to sing.

I am not disappointed in how He runs His universe. Let me go a little further and tell us I was not disappointed in the Lord

- When He saved me from my sins;
- When He lifted me from the miry clay and placed my feet on a solid rock
- When He touched me and made me whole;
- When he delivered me from my enemies;
- When He kept me safe through many a crisis; and
- When He filled me with His wonderful Holy Ghost.

I can tell you this morning that I've never been disappoint in His grace; it has always been sufficient.

I've never been disappointed in His love, it has always been overwhelming.

I've never been disappointed in His word, it has always been dependable.

I've never been disappointed in His promises, they have always been trustworthy.

I've never been disappointed in His blessings, they have always been abundant.

I've never been disappointed in His will for my life, it has always been just right.

I've never been disappointed in His answers to my questions, they have always been correct.

I've never been disappointed in His leadership, it has always been faithful.

And I've never been disappointed in His methods; they have always been proper and timely.

I've got to close this message, but I think I need to tell us that it is not just me who has never been disappointed in our Lord. I don't believe that Zacharius was disappointed when Jesus went to his house to eat.

I don't believe that the woman, who had suffered with an issue of blood, was disappointed when she touched the hem of His garments.

I don't believe that the disciples were disappointed when out on the stormy sea Jesus spoke the words *"Peace be still"* and the storm cleared.

I don't believe the five hundred thousand, plus the women and children, were disappointed when He fed the entire multitude with two fishes and five loves of bread.

I don't believe the blind man was disappointed when he told the critics that asked if He was a sinner—"I don't know, but one thing I do know that whereas I was blind, now I can see.

Time and time again Jesus has proven that He will never disappoint anybody. As the head of the church, you will never be disappointed in Him. As a friend that sticks closer than a brother, you will never be disappointed in Him. Other may—

- Gossip about you—He won't
- Betray your confidence—He won't
- Falsely accuse you—He won't
- Shamefully embarrass you—He won't
- Hold a grudge against you—He won't

And although other may—

- Disregard your feelings—He won't
- Undermine your efforts—He won't
- Corrupt your character—He won't
- Reject your love—He won't

- Misunderstand your situations—He won't
- Discredit your commitment—He won't

You will never be disappointed in Jesus. Jesus had been everything He said He would be. Jesus has gone everywhere He said He would go. Jesus had done everything He said he would do. Jesus had given everything He said He would give.

Just put your trust and full confidence in Him. Wait on Him.

> ### *WHAT YOU CAN ALWAYS EXPECT*
> Scripture: Romans 14:23; Peter 5:8; Malachi 3:6
> Hebrews 12:8; Mark 13:31

"Whatever is not of faith is sin."

Romans 14:23

"Be sober, be vigilant: Because your adversary the devil, as a roaring lion walketh about seeking whom he may devour."

Peter 5:8

"For I am the Lord, I change not."

Malachi 3:6

"Jesus Christ, the same yesterday, today and forever."

Hebrews 13:8

"Heaven and earth shall pass away, but my words shall not pass away."

Mark 13:31

There are many things in life that we can never be absolutely sure of. Permit me to share a few examples. We are never really certain (we never really know for sure) how we may be feeling physically tomorrow even if you feel as fit as a fiddle today; one's skies may be blue and one's day may be filled with sunshine—but it may be a different story on tomorrow; the job you and I have today could well be terminated on tomorrow.

You can never know for sure what you may encounter around the next corner; what will be in the next sealed container you may open; what trials or temptations we may face tomorrow; and we may never know how long we will live in this present life—or who may meet with death in the next few days.

How many times have we been surprised or even shocked at what a day brings forth. How quickly our circumstances can change with just a knock on the door, or with a telephone call, or with a blown fuse, or with a flat tire, or with one stumble in the dark. Even so, there are some things even in this life we can know for sure. I can always expect—and we can be absolutely sure of—pray with me while I talk from this subject—"**What You Can Always Expect**".

It is my custom to share only three thoughts. But today so that I will not have to divide this message into two sermons—I'm going to give you at least five things to think about and I'm through.

I.   **You Can Always Expect Sin To Be Sin**

The Bible says, "all unrighteousness is sin." It also says, "Whatsoever is not of faith is sin." You can always expect sin to be sin. No matter how big or small you may think it to be (like dirt is always dirt, no matter whether it be a thimble full or a tub full); no matter what others may or may not think about it; no matter if others observe you committing it, or if it's done in secret; no matter if it be an action or an attitude, you can expect sin to be sin.

Personal convictions may vary from time to time, but sin is still sin. Although you may color it, or disguise it, or rename it, denounce it, enhance it, ignore it, or even embrace it—sin will always be sin—and there is nothing you, nor I, not anybody else can do about it. You can always expect and depend on sin being sin.

II.   **You Can Always Expect Satan To Be Satan**

Ever since his rebellion against God, Satan has always been and will always be a liar—lying about anything and everything; a deceiver—deceiving whoever, however and whenever; an imitator—

acting as if he were God Himself; a master of manipulation—using people for his own selfish and sinister purposes; an enemy—hating you and constantly trying to destroy you. He is and will always be a critic—who will criticize you about everything you will ever do for God.

Here's how he always operates. He will endeavor to confuse your mind; to harden your heart; to corrupt your conversation; to control your will; and he will always be doing his best to ruin your life. and you never need to expect him to change for the better. He won't and this you can expect, yes, you can always expect sin to be sin and Satan to be Satan.

III. **You Can Always Count On God To Be God**

He continually and eternally remains the same. He never changes—regardless of the time, or place or the occasion; regardless of what has happened or what could have happened, of what man/woman may or may not be involved. of one's personal theology or background or level of intelligence, and regardless of any opposition or contradiction that may develop—God will still be God and you can depend on that.

You can always expect God to be wise in His decisions; to be Holy in His character; to be loyal to His subjects; to be generous in His provisions; to be loving in His discipline; to be righteous in His judgment; and you can always expect God to be true to His word. This you can depend on.

I have said—you can expect sin to be sin—you can expect Satan to be Satan—and you can expect God to always be God; there is someone else—

IV. **You Can Also Depend On Jesus Christ To Always Be Jesus Christ**

The Bible says this about Him—"Jesus Christ, the same yesterday, today and will be forever." What He was—He is—and what He will always be. He is both the Alpha and the Omega, the beginning and the end; the King of Kings and the Lord of Lords; the Son of God and the Son of man; the Rock of Ages—the Lily of the Valley;

the Savior and our Redeemer; our Divine Physician and our Great Refuge.

His message is a message of salvation; His promises are promises of hope; His commandments are commandments of love' His presence is the presence of absolute assurance; His blood is the blood of Divine atonement; His touch is a touch of complete and everlasting satisfaction.

Furthermore Jesus is Master over both wind and waves; is Master over sunshine and rain; is Master over both fear and doubt; is Master over both sickness and disease; and Jesus is Master over both death and the grave. This you can depend on. He knows what to do. He knows how to do it. And He knows who to do it for.

And you can expect sin to always be sin—You can expect Satan to always be Satan—you can expect God to always be God and you can expect Jesus to always be Jesus with a touch of complete and everlasting satisfaction.

V. You Can Expect The Word Of God To Always Be The Word Of God

For it is the final word. Although you may debate it—you can't change it. Although you may despise it—you can't change it. Although you may disagree with it—you can't change it. Although you may defy it—you can't change it. Although you may dispute it—you can't change it. Although you may desecrate it—you can't change it. The Word of God still remains the Word of God.

The Word of God will never change because it has the authority of God behind it; because it has the power of the blood upon it; because it has the glory of eternity within it; and because it has the assurance of victory woven into it.

The Bible says "Heaven and earth shall pass away but my words shall not pass away." I recall during my childhood days in the country when folk used the family Bible to put things in for safe keeping. The Bible is not to put things in—it's to get things out.

LIFE'S GREATEST CHOICE
Scripture: Deuteronomy 30:1-19; Joshua 24:14

"I call heaven and earth as witnesses today against you, that I have set before you life and death, blessing and cursing, therefore choose life, that both you and your descendants may live."

Deuteronomy 30:19

"Now therefore, fear the Lord serve Him in sincerity and in truth, and put away the gods which your fathers served on the other side of the river and in Egypt. Serve the Lord."

Joshua 24:14

Life has been defined as the sum total of a person's choices. From the cradle to the grave we face many great decisions and we are compelled to make many choices. Come to think about it, we make many choices during the waking hours of a single day. For most of us we make the logical and simple choice to get up—or stay in bed, to eat—or not to eat, to go to work—or not go to work, and we make the logical and simple choice to come home after work, or go elsewhere.

There are other choices we make that can be rather complex and painful. With every situation that comes along we make a choice.

- We choose to be kind or rude
- We choose to be friendly or cold
- We choose to be mature or childish
- We choose to be considerate or selfish or
- We choose to be wise or foolish.

There are other choices we can make that will make a difference in our relationship with other people that include those choices of moral value which deals directly with our faithfulness or our honesty, our morality, our loyalty or our commitment. My subject today is about **"Life's Greatest Choice"**.

Someone is now asking "What is life's greatest choice?" I'm glad you asked. I am obliged to tell us—life's greatest choice has to do with

God and our commitment to Him. The Bible presents that choice to us through Joshua, when he says— *"choose you this day whom you will serve."* (Joshua 24:15) You see, we are all servants of God or servants of sin. We are mastered by God's will or our own appetites and desires. Life's greatest choice is made when we decide which master we will serve. Three things I'm going to say about this and I'm through.

I.   **A Necessary Personal Choice**

Note first—because it is life's greatest choice, it is a necessary personal choice. Every person must choose for or against God. To refuse or neglect to make the choice is to make one anyhow. If you don't make a choice—you have decided already to remain in the terrible situation you are in. It's a personal choice. A wife can't make it for her husband—a husband can't make it for his wife.

Although Joshua said, "as for me and my house we will serve the Lord" what he was saying is "I'm going to be such a good example for my family that they too will know the reality of serving a true and living God."

My grandmother used a term when we were growing up "every tub must sit on its own bottom." I didn't understand it then but what she was really saying—we individually are responsible to God and we must individually choose. Of course, there are good choices and bad choices. Let me site a few good choices found in God's word.

- Abraham made a good choice when he chose to sojourn into the land of promise and look for a city whose builder and maker is God.
- Enoch made a good choice when he chose to walk with God and did so for 300 years.
- Joseph made a good choice when he chose to retain his integrity in the foreign country of Egypt.
- The three Hebrews made a good choice when they chose to refuse to bow to the golden idol of the king, regardless to the penalty for not doing so.

- Matthew made a good choice when he chose to leave his tax collecting job and follow the Lord.

Life's greatest choice is a necessary personal choice.

II. An Urgent Choice

Life is so uncertain—but death is sure. Since we have no guarantee of tomorrow, we had better do what we ought to do today.

Two trains used to leave the railway station in Chicago at the same time. For seven miles they ran side by side. Then their tracks turned and went in opposite directions.

One train went west and ended up at the Pacific Coast. The other went east and arrived in New York City. The trains ran side by side at first, but ended up with a continent separating them.

Two men can begin life side by side. Live next door to each other—play together—attend the same school—join the same Boy Scout Troop. After a few years one makes a decision to accept and follow Christ—the other does not. One follows the pathway that leads to righteousness—the other follows the path of sin and destruction. One will one day land in Heaven—the other will end up in the awful torment of Hell.

How careful we should be to choose the right way. It is urgent that one choose Jesus—the way to Heaven. Life's greatest choice—is a necessary, personal choice and it is also an urgent choice.

And there's one more thing I want to say about—Life's Greatest Choice.

III. It's A Logical Choice

When you and I consider all that God has done and is doing for us we ought to want to serve Him. We ought to choose to serve Him because He is a very personal God. That is—He reveals himself to us on a one on one basis; He fellowships with us personally. He walks with us and talks with us. We can get to know Him intimately and enjoy being in His presence. He's a faithful God. A God you can trust. God will never let you down—He shall supply all your needs.

God never lets you off.

I was flying one night aboard one of those big airline planes. The plane began to be tossed rather violently. Then the pilot said—"Friends, we are entering a slight turbulence." Up there I didn't think any turbulence is slight. Even so, he said "We are now flying—15,000 feet—we are going up to 20,000 feet, to get over the weather." The plane turned upward and soon we are smooth flying again.

The thought came to me as I sat there with my seat belt fastened. I thought about how many times I had hit those turbulent spots in my life. If I looked toward Heaven and got a little closer to God, it's wonderful how things smooth out. Who wouldn't serve a God like that? It is a logical choice—to serve a God who never fails.

I read this incident the other day that told about the care of our God. It was about an elderly couple—a man and his wife who lived in a little cottage. Times were hard and they needed money. They borrowed money. They were forced to use their little cottage as security for the debt. The time came for them to pay back the money. But they had no money.

One day a lawyer came to that cottage to tell these old people they had to move out. The house was being sold for payment for the debt. The wife of the couple told that lawyer—"We will do what you say, but give us time to talk to God about it." The lawyer told her to go ahead. She got down on her knees and talked to God like she was born and raised with Him. Here are some of the words she told the lord.

She reminded God that they were His children. They told God how hard it would be for them to make it with nowhere to live in their old age. She quoted some of the precious promises from the Bible telling how safe God's children are who trust in Him. Last of all she prayed God's blessings on those who wanted to take her little house away.

The lawyer heard her prayer. He turned away from the door and quietly went to the owner who had sent him to tell the couple to move out. He told the owner, "I couldn't serve them papers after I heard that woman pray." He said, "My Mother had faith in that same God and trusted Him for everything. I just couldn't do it." The owner who sent him there said, "My Mother trusted in that same God. Go back in the morning—tell that couple that little cottage is theirs. They can stay there as long as they live."

Won't God do it? Won't He make a way?

> ## LIVE CLOSER IN GOOD TIMES AND IN BAD
> Scripture: Job 35:10

"But no one says, where is God, my maker, who gives songs in the night."

Job 35:10

We, as believers, need to be established firmly upon the rock of truth and Christian experience. Christ must be alive and real within our hearts, or we will most certainly be upset, confused and led astray by situations and circumstances with which we will be confronted. Only a vital faith in God can hold a person during the time of a crisis.

Human nature doesn't seem to have changed radically through the centuries. We are much like poor old Job—often wondering why tragedy must strike us; why disappointment and trouble must come our way. We also often wonder why life for us does not hold a constant pattern of happiness and blessings.

But, life means change; and change calls for the ability to adapt ourselves to circumstances. Life is not all sunshine—God never meant it to be. But thank God it is not all storm and shadow. Some days must be dark and dreary.

My subject today is a bit of spiritual advice—even a challenge to believers—"**Live Closer In Good Times And Bad Times**"

Job was not the last to inquire in the time of trouble—*"Where is God my maker?"* But he is the one who asked—*"Where is my maker who gives songs in the night?"*

Never expect the thrill of victory without the effort of conquest. It doesn't work that way. Walk with Him in the day and you will find it much easier to sing with Him in the long night of trouble. I repeat, my subject today is "**Live Closer In Good Times And In Bad**".

Three things I'm going to say about this, and I'm through.

I. **We Cannot Avoid The Hard Places In Life**

Can I tell us that we cannot avoid the hard places in life no matter how hard we try? There are reasons for this. Hardship is a necessary condition for growth. Paul wrote to the believers in Rome—*"Tribulations worketh patience"*: (Romans 5:3)

We desire the patience, but dread the tribulation which makes for its development. An acorn is not an oak as it drops from the parent tree to the ground. It takes time—a great amount of it—hot summers, cold winters, frost and rain, and being buried to make an acorn into an oak.

Ask a giant oak "How did you become so stately and big?" It would tell us "I did it by growing a little wood every day."

A tiny bird must leave the safety of its nest and try its own wings. Life means struggle as well as change.

All of us, in the course of a lifetime, will encounter serious problems and difficulties—some of which may be of major proportions. But it is all necessary for the building and strengthening of our character.

When the violinist tightens the pegs, he is not trying to break the strings but to tune it with the rest of the instruments and the rest of the orchestra.

Do you feel that life is, or has been, hard on you? Really what is happening to you has been happening to folk like you (to all humanity) for thousands of years. Some, according to the record, fared far worse. Many of them were better people than we ever will be. Permit me to mention a few.

Remember Daniel—that fine, resolute, godly man who faithfully lived for God. His faith was responsible for getting him into trouble even to the point of getting him thrown into a den of lions. Daniel turned this problem into a means of everlasting glory.

In the days of Zedekiah, Jeremiah was thrust into a dungeon, deep and muddy, in the courtyard of a Jerusalem prison. But it was this very experience which gave him a coveted opportunity to proclaim the will of the Lord to the king.

We cannot avoid the hard places in life, no matter how hard we try.

II. **Be Prepared To Face A Variety Of Changes**

My second though is this—he who takes his stand for Christ and travels resolutely toward a heavenly goal, must be prepared to face a variety of changing circumstances.

I've said it many times—the Lord brings us through it to get us to it. As we go forward with God, we ought to learn better how to handle the woes and hard places of life. As we grow, God will trust us with heavier burdens and larger responsibilities.

I learned this lesson early in my ministry. I find myself passing it on to the younger ministers God has blessed me to minister to. The Bible tells us—*"Not to despise the day of small things"*. (Zechariah 4:10). We must learn to crawl before we can walk, and walk before we can run.

Every year should bring the Christian to a great maturity in things of the spirit. We ought to become more capable and trustworthy in carrying out God's orders. Our goal should be to draw closer to God. Sometimes this is done at great personal cost. We should not despise the hard times and the trials that might come our way and fall our lot. A bit of opposition is good for us.

Kites rise into the wind—not with it. Sailors tell us a head wind is much better than no wind at all. Hardship is the native soil of manhood, self reliance, and strength. We need to learn to accept whatever comes with quiet confidence in God.

Never fret over what you cannot help, to do so is but a waste of good time and energy. What you can help, if you can help it, go to work on it. Either way, you must trust in God to bring you out. Remember—he who takes a stand for Christ and travels resolutely toward a heavenly goal, must be prepared to face a variety of changing circumstances.

III. Live Close To Him

In this message today, I have attempted to challenge us to live closer in good times and in bad times, and my final thought is this. God can give you songs in the night if you live close to Him.

During a violent storm at sea, a passenger said to a ten year old boy, "Aren't you afraid this ship might just sink?"

The lad replied—"Naw, I'm not scared. My father's at the wheel and he's an experienced sailor. He has brought many ships through the fiercest storms."

Years ago a fifteen year old lad was on a ship far out a sea. The captain ordered the lad to climb to the top of the mask-head. The ship was rolling and the boy was frightened. Half way up, he looked down at the captain and said, "I'm afraid I'm going to fall."

But the captain, wise in such matters, said—"Don't look down, look up and keep on climbing."

That is the way to wage a successful war against encroaching circumstances. Look up and keep climbing. God can give you and me a song in the night, if we live close to Him. If trouble should come—as it most assuredly will—sing in spite of it. Even the wind and the waves obey the Son of God. He who notes the fall of each sparrow will certainly take care of you.

I close with this—A man, visiting a friend's house, noticed a picture of Jesus hanging on his wall. The eyes on the picture looked like they were looking right at him. This made the man so uncomfortable that he moved across the room. It still appeared to look right at him. He said to his host, "Doesn't that make you uncomfortable?"

His friend said, "No—the picture tells me God loves me so much that He can't keep His eyes off of me."

Because He couldn't keep his eyes off me, He went to Calvary and there died to take away all my sins.

WHAT DO YOU DO WHEN YOU ARE CRITICIZED FOR DOING WHAT YOU KNOW IS RIGHT
Scripture: John12:1-5

"Then Mary took a pound of very costly oil of spikenard, anointed the feet of Jesus, and wiped His feet with her hair. And the house was filled with the fragrance of the oil. But one of His disciples, Judas Iscariot, Simon's son, who would betray Him, said, 'Why was this fragrant oil not sold for three hundred denari and given to the poor?'"

John 12:3-5

We are living at a time and in a society where there is more pressure upon folk to do that which we know to be wrong, than there is to do that which we know is right. Wrong doing has become so commonplace, sinful living and immoral conduct has become so acceptable, that the time honored virtues, such as honesty, integrity and common decency have seemingly gone out of style.

In this society in which we live, it is possible for one to encounter more criticism for doing what is right than you will for doing that which is wrong. This trend is true in every facet of society. People who break the law seem to be more popular than those who obey the law. Folk who are kind, nice and courteous are looked upon as odd-balls; while those who are mean, selfish and over-bearing are looked upon as role-models.

In our society, now-a-days, folk who play by the rules and do that which is right, will be criticized by their peers and looked upon as being weak, scared and not a member of the <u>What's Happening Now Generation.</u> This trend spills over into the work-place. Employees who take pride in their work, and put in a full day's work for a full day's pay are looked down upon by those fellow workers who do shoddy work and get by doing as little as possible.

Would you believe it if I told you this same trend can be found in the church? Yes, even the church—that agency which is founded upon the principle of doing those things that are right; even in the church—the citadel of righteousness, you can sometimes get raked over the coals for merely doing what you know to be right. So the question we want to attempt to answer in this message today is "What do you do when you are criticized for doing what you know is right?"

At least three thoughts I wish to share and I'm through.

I.   People Who Do What Is Right Expose Those Who Do Half Way Right

People who are committed pull the cover off of those who just come along for the ride. People who love the Lord, their church and their Pastor and who really love the fellow members of the church are sometimes branded as preacher lovers—or religious fanatics. And so, if you are growing in grace, if you are becoming more involved in the total program of the church, if you are bent on doing that which you know to be right, get ready to be criticized.

You might be lied on, spied on, verbally abused and falsely accused. You see, people who do that which is right expose those who do 'half-way right."

And I'm hoping in this message today to answer an all important question—**What do you do when you are criticized for doing what you know is right.**

II.   Doing What Is Right Is Practical Today

My next thought is this—This idea of being criticized for doing that which is right is practical today—and it started many centuries ago. There was Abel, the second son of Adam and Eve. He did that which was right by giving an acceptable sacrifice to God and as a result, he was not only criticized but killed by his own brother. Then there was Joseph, the eleventh son of Jacob. He did what was right by refusing the romantic advances of Potiphar's wife and he was not only criticized by Mrs. Potiphar, he was thrown in jail and served a twelve year sentence.

In today's message, we have a woman named Mary, the sister of Martha and Lazarus, whose love for Jesus was so strong that she put herself in line to be the object of harsh and severe criticism. Mary was a member of a family which was very close to Jesus. They lived in Bethany, a little town located near Jerusalem. Every time Jesus went to Bethany, He stayed in their home.

Jesus had befriended Mary and Martha by bringing their brother back to life after he had been in a grave four days. Lazarus was walking around alive again because of the love, compassion and the miraculous power of Jesus Christ. Mary, Martha and Lazarus could sing the song with more meaning than anyone, "Oh How I love Jesus—because He first loved me."

On this occasion, Mary and Martha gave a banquet in Jesus' honor. They wanted to show Jesus how much they loved Him. They wanted His disciples, and all the citizens of Bethany to know the place He had in their hearts. The people flocked there in large numbers. Mary had made up her mind, many days before this banquet, what she was going to do to let Jesus know how special He was to her. While all the guests were seated at the banquet table— Mary walked in and went over to the place where Jesus was seated. In her hand she held a costly bottle of perfume. She had taken a large portion of her life's savings to purchase it. Despite her personal sacrifice, she wanted only the best for Jesus.

She knew that she would be accused of being extravagant, but she knew that true love is extravagant and true love has no limits. So right there in the Banquet Hall, before all those distinguished guests, Mary took the cap off this expensive bottle of perfume, got down on knees, poured the perfume over his feet, then wiped his feet with her hair—and the Bible says, *"the sweet smelling fragrance filled the entire room."* Everything which had gone on was right. The idea was right. The guest of honor was right. Honoring Jesus, her Lord and Savior, by expressing her love extravagantly was right. Everybody knew it was right. But wait a minute, there is always one negative voice in the crowd.

While all of the rejoicing was going on, there was one fellow who had his mouth poked out. Of all the people to be angry—it was one of His Disciples. Jesus had fed him when he was hungry and had done everything for him he had done for the other Disciples—even more. He was made treasurer of the group. He tells Mary, "You had no business doing all that. That perfume could have been sold—given to me to help the poor. You went overboard Mary. You think you are right but you are wrong."

Jesus felt it necessary to come to Mary's rescue. As Judas was ranting and raving—Jesus spoke up and said—*"Let her alone. Judas, sit down and shut up. It is easier to be critical than it is to be correct. This dear lady has done a wonderful thing. She has symbolically anointed me for my burial. I won't be around very long—the poor you will have with you always. Because of what she has done, her name will go down in Biblical History. In centuries to come, wherever the gospel is preached—the name of Mary will be exalted because of her extravagant display of love and affection for the Lord."*

Yes Mary was criticized for doing what she knew was right—and she was defended for her actions by Jesus Christ, himself.

III. **When You Know You Are Right—Keep on Doing What You Are Doing**

Before I finish this message—let's look back at my initial question. I ask again—**What do you do when you are criticized for doing what you know is right?** The first thing to do is to be sure your action is approved by God and endorsed by the Holy Spirit; then recognize the criticism you receive from doing right is the work of Satan; and finally, here is the third thing—when you know you are right—just keep on doing what you are doing.

- If you have been praying—keep on praying.
- If you have been singing—keep on singing.
- If you have been trusting—keep on trusting.
- It you have been witnessing—keep on witnessing.
- If you have been praising His name—keep on praising His name.

CHAPTER VIII

"Wherefore, brethren, look ye out among you seven men of honest report, full of the Holy Ghost and wisdom, whom we may appoint over this business. But we will give ourselves continually to prayer, and to the ministry of the Word."

Acts 6:3-4

Knowing that he had come to Tulsa to help Reverend Dotson with his pastoral work at Mt. Zion, young George Calvin McCutchen also knew that he must become a part of all of the Church's activities. This included the District activities of which Mt. Zion was a participant. Therefore, during the third week of August 1953, when the Creek District Baptist Sunday School and B.T.U. Congress (now known as the Creek District Baptist Association) convened at the First Baptist Church, Sand Springs, George accompanied Reverend and Mrs. J. H. Dotson to the meetings, where they introduced this newcomer to the congress body.

Reverend A. L. Branch, Pastor of Paradise Baptist Church Tulsa and Moderator of the District, invited young McCutchen to speak in some of the sessions. Inspired by his manner and his messages, Reverend Branch assigned this new arrival to the District the task of being an instructor in the Creek District Congress, teaching one class in both the morning and afternoon sessions.

Over the years, any Biblical course that no one else was available to teach seemingly was given to Reverend McCutchen. He has taught such classes as—

- Baptist Doctrine
- The Church Through the Centuries
- How to Read and Study the Bible

- The New Testament—It's Contents and Values
- The Role Of The Deacon In The Black Baptist Church

The next year Reverend McCutchen was honored by his peers when he was elected to serve as President of the Pastor's Conference. Succeeding the late Dr. T. Oscar Chappelle, Sr., who had become Vice-Moderator-At-Large, Reverend McCutchen served as Pastor's Conference President for ten years.

Reverend McCutchen was offered positions such as Recording Secretary and Corresponding Secretary—positions that he refused to accept, but four years later accepted the position of Treasurer, which he held for twenty years.

In 1983, Reverend McCutchen's name was submitted by the nominating committee of the Creek District Association to serve as Moderator. During this session, Reverend McCutchen received the majority vote and became the new Moderator, succeeding Reverend LeRoy K. Jordan.

During the seven years Dr. McCutchen served as Moderator of the Creek District Baptist Association, he traveled throughout the District helping pastors and churches as he could. Under his leadership, the District initiated and completed the rebuilding and refurbishing of Camp Davis.

> *"I gave up the Moderator position for three reasons. First, I had been elected to become President of the Oklahoma Baptist State Convention, and to adequately fill both positions would require more energy and put demands on my time that I could not give. Secondly, I believe those who follow leaders should be given a chance to move up; and thirdly, I wanted to get to heaven when I die."*

When Dr. McCutchen resigned as Creek District Moderator, he was offered the position of *"Moderator Emeritus"*—a position that he refused. The new Moderator, Dr. Bertrand Bailey, instead named a Bible Conference in his honor. Each year, on the first Saturday in March (a date near Dr. McCutchen's birthday of March 1), Creek District met at the Mt. Zion Baptist Church for the *"G. Calvin McCutchen Sr. Bible Study Conference"*.

He was also named by Moderator Bailey as *Chief Advisor* of the Association, and conducted the Minister's Seminars for the Congress of Christian Education.

In 2001 Mt. Zion Baptist Church and several other churches in the area saw the need to break away from the Creek District Association and started the First United District Baptist Association. Dr. McCutchen took the role as Senior Advisor to the Association.

One Of The Whosoevers, this young farm boy and minister came to the District 54 years ago, and made a dynamic mark. For his outstanding service, leadership, and concerns, he received plaques from Calvary Baptist Church, Sapulpa; Timothy Baptist Church, Tulsa; and the Creek District Association.

> ## THE PURPOSE FOR LIVING
> Scripture: Philippians 1:20-21

"The thing I want and hope for is that I will not fail Christ in anything. I hope I will have the courage now as always to show the greatest of Christ in my life here on earth. I want to do that if I die or live. To me the only thing about living is Christ."

Philippians 1:20-21a

A writer unknown to me has said, "There are two great moments in every person's life. The first is when you are born; the second is when you discover why you were born."

I believe we were all born for a reason, and it is our responsibility to discover that reason and redirect our lives towards God's ultimate purpose for our lives. Every one of us (and I mean everyone) has a purpose for living. With that though firmly fixed in our minds, permit me to share a few thoughts the Devine Spirit has given to me.

First, I think I should tell us that God has a higher calling on each of our lives. Your calling, as well as mine, will call you. It will be a calling to realize your full potential in every aspect of your life. A calling is a difficult concept to explain. It's something like Louis Armstrong's description of Jazz. "Man, if you can't explain it, you don't know what it is, but you will know what it is when you see, hear and feel it. And, you will feel it in your heart before you know it in your head."

I ought to tell us that the seeds of our future could be planted in the fields of our past. But what lies ahead of us and what lies before us are small matters compared to what lies within us. Let's agree on this important fact—every one of us has a purpose for living. And with that in mind, I want to ask you something that is very important. "**What Is Your Purpose In Life?**"

I would like to show us from God's word what our purpose in life should be. It is obvious that many are living their lives for the wrong purposes.

I.   Some People Live For Pleasure

I said some live for pleasure, but it would be more accurate to say that many wake up in the morning with but one thing on their mind—to seek pleasure wherever they can find it. There is nothing wrong with pleasure. Someone has said our religion was not designed to make our pleasures less, but there is something wrong when all that a society cares about is pleasure.

Many of our precious young people have been brain-washed into believing their every waking moment should be spent seeking pleasure. They spend their lives seeking pleasure among their friends. When they are alone they have to be watching television and hearing music. Their every waking moment has got to be fun time. Life is not to be taken as one big party; life is a mixture of many things. The Bible recommends that we live a balanced life.

A very wise man wrote "To everything there is a season and a time to every purpose under the Heaven; a time to weep and a time to laugh—a time to mourn and a time to dance."

Many a man thinks he is buying pleasure when he is really selling himself as a slave to it. We should not live for pleasure.

II. **Some People Live For Popularity**

You can ask people in our society—

- Why do you have those things in your ears?
- Why do you drink alcoholic beverages?
- Why do you do drugs/
- And fellows why do you wear your pants so low that they look like they are going to fall off?

Ask them why do they do the things they do, and their answer to the question is simple. They got involved in these things because they wanted to please the crowd they hung out with and because everyone else is doing it.

When some of us older folk were growing up, we were taught to think for ourselves. In our society today where many live their lives for the wrong purposes, all we have is a bunch of carbon copies.

God individually created us all differently for a very special reason. It is better to be right than to be popular. Popularity is the purpose of the world. We should not live for popularity.

III. **Some People Live For Pride**

Some people get up in the morning and the one thing they seek to do that day is to make an effort to impress the people they associate with. They do it in a variety of ways. They drive cars they can't afford. They live in homes and in neighborhoods far beyond their means.

It is so easy for Christians to fall short of God's best because we are so proud. When we are proud, we discount the need for God in our lives. Proud people tend to alienate others, even their friends. Pride can be a stumbling block from receiving God's blessings.

Pride almost kept Naaman from being healed of his leprosy. Pride and disobedience can keep us from God's answers for us.

If you must be proud, be proud of your church. The person who is not proud of his or her church seldom makes the church proud of him or her. Man's pride and God's glory cannot co-exist. The

Bible says, *"Pride goeth before destruction, and a haughty spirit before a fall."*

IV.   Some People Live As Paul Did

So we have said some people live for pleasure, some people live for popularity, some people live for pride—but, thank God, some people live as Paul did. Paul had one purpose in life. What was it? In the text it is plainly stated—*"For me to live is Christ".*

The Everyday Bible quotes Paul as saying—*"The thing I want and hope for is that I will not fail Christ in anything."* He continues to say—*"I hope I have the courage now as always to show the greatest of Christ in my life while I'm on this earth. And I want to do that if I die or if I live. To me the only thing about living is Christ."*

Paul's purpose in life was to live for Christ. Paul looked for ways he could serve Christ. One day while traveling the road to Damascus, Paul turned a corner and met Jesus. This was the most important thing that ever happened in his life.

He was on his way to persecute Christ's Church and God halted him in his wild career. A light brighter than the noonday sun shone about him; it blinded his eyes; and he fell from his beast and cried out, *"Lord, what wilt thou have me to do?"*

Paul gives the secret of his success in the Christian life. He stated, *"I was not disobedient to the Heavenly vision."* Wherever he went he claimed to know nothing among the people he served, but Christ and Him crucified. He said such things as his testimony—*"I'm crucified with Christ, nevertheless I live—and yet not I that live, it is the Christ that lives in me. I am saved in the cross of our Lord and Savior, Jesus Christ."*

My challenge to us today is consecration and light. Anyone can go through the outward motions of religion, but a true Christian is one in whose heart there burns the bright flame of faith in Jesus Christ.

It is reported that a man was killed one night at a railroad crossing. His relatives sued the railroad, claiming negligence on the part of the watchman. During the ensuing trial, the watchman was called to the witness stand. The prosecuting attorney asked several question—were you on duty at the time of the accident; did you have a lantern. To all of these questions the watchman answered in the affirmative and his testimony helped the railroad to win their case.

An officer of the railroad came to the watchman to thank him for giving evidence in their favor. He also asked him to tell him why he was so nervous while they questioned him. The watchman's reply was—"I feared any moment that the attorney would ask was the lantern lit".

COMMITTED TO THE HIGHWAYS AND HEDGES
Scripture: Luke 14:1-23

"And the Lord said unto the servant, go out into the highway and hedges and compel them to come in that my house may be filled."

Luke 14:23

Commitment is a wonderful word. Some of the smartest people in the world have built their lives around it. For example—there are athletes who built their lives around being committed to a certain sport. There are musicians that have built their lives being committed to playing a certain kind of instrument. And there are skilled workers who have built their lives around being the best in their trade.

There are times when commitment is not good. Some people are committed to doing evil. The things we have committed our life to doing tell a great deal about us. This would be a terrible world if we did not have people who live a committed life. Where would God's church be today if it were not for Christians who have committed themselves to the causes of Jesus Christ? The church has reached millions around the world with the gospel because committed Christians have sent and are sending missionaries around the world sharing the good news that Jesus came to seek and to save. the subject I have selected to speak from today is "<u>Committed To The Highways And The Hedges</u>".

Normally we do not think of turning to Jesus for advice on how to throw a party. We look to Him for advice on how to pray, how to fix a broken heart, how to understand the sacred scriptures, even how to face death. But most of us, believe that Jesus and parties don't mix. We identify Jesus with good news but not with good times. But the problem is ours not His.

This Gospel of Luke and the scriptures I have selected to speak from today is our best guide to the social life of our Lord. The text is taken from an occasion, and it tells us the kind of invitation that is extended when Jesus throws a party. *"And the Lord said unto the servant, go out into the highway and hedges and compel them to come in that My house may be filled."*

As a church—as concerned followers—as Believers—we should be committed to the highways and hedges for several reasons.

I.   To Receive Food And Fellowship

First it's because the invitation is extended for folk to receive food and fellowship. *"Supper"* is a mealtime, but more than that it is a time for fellowship with those we love most dearly. Supper is still the best time of the day around any house. It means laughter and joy. It means satisfying the body but also the soul.

Coming to God is like that. God invites folk to divine food and fellowship. Our Lord extends an invitation not a subpoena. We can go out and invite people but we cannot make them come. Somewhere between here and there they must decide for themselves.

This brings me to another reason we need to be committed to the highway and hedges—

II.   The Invitation Can Be And Is So Easily Declined

Folk can so easily give what they believe to be an excuse for not coming. There is a difference between an excuse and a reason. We give an excuse when we have no reason to offer.

In this parable our Lord is careful to point out that when God threw a party, and an invitation was given to at least three—each one had an excuse. One said 'He just bought some land.' It could not be properly inspected at night. The other said he had bought a yoke of oxen and had to prove them. And anyone knows he couldn't best prove them at night. The other was a little more sensible than the others—he said, 'I just got married.' Doubtless the guests could have brought his wife along. But he, like the others, gave an excuse for not doing what he knew he ought to do.

Two begged to be excused. One simply said—'I cannot come!' It matters not how one declines, he is still saying no to God's invitation. Even though many decline the invitation we are yet to be committed to the highway and the hedges because the Lord tells us to compel them that His house might be full.

There is yet another reason we should be committed to the highway and the hedges ...

III. Our Lord Extends An Invitation To All Who Are Hungry

There will always be those who do not hunger and thirst after righteousness, but it is equally true that there are those who do and will respond. Christ, in this parable, tells us not to restrict our invitation list to your kind. Mix it up, invite the poor, maimed, lame and the blind. Don't invite only those who will reciprocate by inviting you to their parties.

There is an urgency in the invitation. Christ said, "Compel them to come." Why this note of urgency? It is because of the need of those who are invited. We have all sinned and 'the wages of sin is death.' It is urgent that we respond quickly because the invitation will not always be extended. God warns that His spirit will not always strive with man.

Isaiah 55:6 admonishes 'seek ye the Lord while He may be found, call ye upon Him while He is near.' Note how anxious the host of the feast was to fill his banquet hall. He was prepared to use any and every legitimate means at his disposal to get the people in. Still he shut out those who showed no desire or appreciation for his hospitality. "Compel them to come in that my house may be filled."

There is a place set for everyone. All we need to do is accept the invitation. It would be well for us to remember we are not saved by works, but for works. God does not tell us to work hard and earn our way to Heaven. He gives us heaven as a free gift of His grace and expects us to live up to His expectations and our responsibilities. Jesus never glorified laziness or idleness. The Bible says—"He went about daily good."

A man complained to his minister about the injustices and evils in the world. He further blamed God for the mess and said, "I could make a better world myself."

Quietly the minister responded, 'since you could make a better world yourself, good! Go to it! That's exactly what God put you in this world to do."

Our challenge is to be committed to the hedges and highways.

CLAIMING THE BEST THAT LIFE HAS TO OFFER
Scripture: John 10:1-10

"I am come that they may have life, and that they may have it more abundantly."

John 10:10

In very many instances, folk are largely governed by what they think of life. Some folk live for the present, caring only for what they can get and enjoy today. Others have a broader view of life when he thinks of tomorrow as well as today, and when he thinks of eternity as well as time.

I think you will agree with me when I say, when folk believe in and work for a future good in Christ with all their hearts and take the broad outlook they have a deeper and larger interest in life. It is then they become co-workers with God; they care about what He thinks, they are lifted up themselves and they uplift others.

One thing we all have in common is that we all want the best this life has to offer. Another thing we all have in common is that we all have but two lives we can pick from while seeking for the best. We can choose the life that Satan offers us or we can choose the life offered to us by our Lord. I am here to tell us this day that the best life we can have is having Christ in your life. It was He, Himself who said "I have come that they may have life, and have it more abundantly."

Pray with me while I share with you this important thought—when Christ is in your life, you have the best that life has to offer. This I say for several reasons.

I. **We Have A Hedge Around Us**

Job is an example of having a hedge of protection. Satan came before God one day thousands of years ago. We don't have all the words of that conversation, but we have some of the conversation in scripture. The Lord said to Satan 'Whence cometh thou?' Satan answered the Lord and said, "from going to and fro in earth, and from walking up and down in it."

God knew Satan's only purpose is getting God's people to fall into sin. Job's name entered the conversation. The Lord said to Satan, "Have you considered my servant Job?" Satan's response was "Job don't fear You for nothing. You got a hedge of protection around him. Move that hedge and he will curse You to your face."

God knew better. God knew that Job was serving Him because He had blessed him. Job was serving God because he loved Him. God took down the hedge. God allowed the hedge momentarily to be taken down. And everything that could go wrong went wrong for Job. Even so, Job stayed with the Lord.

I need to tell somebody today—the reason you are doing as well as you are today—God has built a hedge around us and Satan can't lay a finger on us unless God allows it. Because of the Lord, we have the best life has to offer—a hedge around us—and

II. **We Have A Hand Under Us**

There used to be an ad for All State Insurance that pictured a family standing in a pair of very large hands. The caption was "You are in good hands with Allstate."

Maybe yes and maybe no—but, the best hands you can be in are the hands of the Lord Jesus Christ. John quotes Jesus—saying, "And I give unto them eternal life, and they shall never perish, neither shall any man pluck them out of my hands."

We need to understand how big His hands are. Isaiah tells us He has measured the waters in the hollow of his hands, and meted out heaven with the span, and comprehended the dust of the earth in a measure, and weighed the mountains in scales and the hills in a balancer. God has measured out the Heavens with the span of His hand. That's how big His hand is. The Bible says—"God has vowed, no man can pluck us out of His "hand"—singular—He don't have to use both hands, just one.

He has placed us in His hand—we have the best life has to offer. A Hedge around us—A Hand under us and

III. A Helper About Us

When the Lord was here on earth, His disciples did not want to see Him go. When He indeed went back to His Father—He said, "I will not leave you comfortless. I will send another comforter, who will abide with you forever." And what a comfort it is to know that we have the Lord with us to teach us and to watch over us! The Holy Spirit is our help with us each day.

The early church had a helper. He was their partner in ministry. The Holy Spirit watched over them. Only when we get to heaven will we find out how often God, the Holy Spirit had opened and shut doors because He knew what was best for us. Yes, we have a Hedge around us—a Hand under us—and a Helper about us. And we have more

IV. We Have A Hope Above Us

Suppose I told you that I was going to inherit enough wealth that would enable me to live a life of luxury and joy like no man on earth has ever lived. You might say—Preacher that's only wishful thinking. But I can assure you that it is not "wishful thinking."

It is the hope that every child of God has. We, like the Apostle Paul, can declare—"Henceforth there is laid up for me a crown of righteousness, which the Lord, the righteous judge shall give me at that day and not to me only, but to all them also that love His appearing."

Lost men—those not in Christ do not have a thing to look forward to. He knows he is only one heartbeat away from eternal damnation. But we who know Jesus have Hope Above Us.

In closing let me remind us that the trouble with most people is they believe too little about ourselves. God put each life on this earth for a purpose.

NO PERFECT SITUATION IN THIS OUR IMPERFECT WORLD
Scripture: Psalm 118:24

"This is the day which the Lord hath made; we will rejoice and be glad in it."

Psalm 118:24

Many folk today have the Utopian complex. It's a term used by psychologists and psychiatrists to describe those people who go through life looking for the perfect situation. They are constantly waiting for the perfect moment to do what they should and ought to do, and to be what they ought to be. In the meanwhile life passes them by and they end up frustrated, feeling betrayed, empty and miserable.

Permit me to springboard this message by sharing an experience from the past that illustrates this fact. It is reported that in the early days of our country, a Native American princess went one morning to visit a neighboring tribe. This tribe was noted for its magnificent fields of corn. The corn they produced each harvest was second to none.

This princess asked the Chief of the tribe for at least one ear of corn that she might take it back for her tribe's seed corn the next year. Graciously her request was granted—with one condition. She could make her choice as she walked down one row. She could not turn back to pick an ear of corn she had already passed. Off she went walking down the row looking for the perfect ear of corn. As she walked, looked and pondered, she could not bring herself to pick an ear, fearing she might find a better one farther down the row. All of a sudden she realized that she had reached the end of her row because she was looking for the perfect ear of corn. She had blown her opportunity. There was no turning back—thus she went back to her tribe empty-handed.

What a parable of life for each of us. Can I tell you that each day God gives us is a generous gift from our all-wise provider? Each day comes with its opportunities that we will never see again. If we wait to select the perfect opportunity, one that will benefit us most, many opportunities will pass you by. If you wait to support the perfect cause, you will not contribute to anything. If you wait to find the perfect job, you will remain unemployed the remainder of your entire life. If you spend your time trapped in that Utopian complex looking for the perfect situation, I got some terrible news for you—it will never come. The simple point I am attempting to make is—"**There Are No Perfect Situations—Ours Is An imperfect world**".

This is the message of the Psalmist. He tells us—don't wait around for another day. Today is the only day we can be sure of. Therefore, we should accept this day with gratitude. We should embrace this day with joy. Commit your life to Christ this day. Say when you read the death notices in the morning paper and yours is not listed among them—"This is the day which the Lord has made—we will rejoice and be glad in it." Acknowledging this one important fact—there are no perfect situations—because ours is an imperfect world.

I'm about through with this message—but there are three observations I want to make in support of this subject and I'm through.

I.   **There Are No Perfect People**

The sooner we learn this, and accept this important fact the better off we will be. There was only one perfect person who ever lived on the face of this earth—and His perfection threatened folk so much they put Him to death. Even so, there are folk who are looking for the perfect mate, the perfect boss, the perfect neighbor and the perfect friend. But there are no perfect people.

A minister friend of mine said for folk he "hung out with—even bothered to visit with, or allow to visit him, he put them through a 'virtue test,' until he realized how unchristian that was. Folk do that today. We have our favorite virtue we test folk by—such as the drink test—the lie test—and the gossip test. If they don't measure up we have a hard time working with them. We mark them off our list. The only trouble with this is many folk have a standard set for others they do not measure up to themselves. What if every time we failed—God marked us off? Thank God He doesn't work that way.

As perfect as God is, He has chosen to work with and through imperfect people. There are no perfect people. There are no perfect situations—because ours is an imperfect world.

II. **There Are No Perfect Marriages**

If you observe a marriage that appears to be perfect, you can rest assured that both man and woman are working at it. Marriages are made in Heaven, but they have to be worked out here on earth. One reason I say there are no perfect marriages—it would mean a perfect man and a perfect woman and both of them being perfect twenty-four hours a day.

I ran across a college classmate who was almost as old as I was—who had never been married. I asked him the reason for this. He said he had missed out on marriage because he was always looking for the right woman. He left it open for me to really dig into his personal business. I said, 'you mean in 50 years you never found the right woman?' His reply was 'can I tell you I found the right one many times, the problem was she was looking for the right man.'

In our imperfect world there are no perfect people and no perfect marriages.

III. **There Are No Perfect Churches**

In our world and in the times which we live—there are "Church Tasters." They are constantly searching for the perfect church and the perfect time to join, and when they do join it is no longer perfect.

Some time ago I preached a sermon I called, "The Chief Trouble in the Church." In that message I pointed out many of the troubles found in churches today. They went from prayerlessness—to lack of commitment—to the church's program—to sermons with no biblical content. But I closed the message by stating that the chief trouble in Christ's church today—it's you and I who are in it.

Each one of us ought to make it our theme song—*"It's me, it's me, it's me o Lord that stands in the need of prayer."* There are very few things in life that really matter—love, compassion, integrity, honesty, commitment, kindness, trust, morality, thoughtfulness, decency and ethics. God placed the church in the world with all of her imperfections to remind us of the real priorities and values of life.

So what—there may not be perfect situations in this life—there is good news. When it comes to faith, God's perfect grace can redeem and restore and love. Our hope is in God's perfect love.

HAVING A MIND TO DO THE LORD'S WORK
Scripture: Nehemiah 4:6

"So we built the wall, and the entire wall was joined together up to half its height, for the people had a mind to work."

Nehemiah 4:6

Belief always proceeds and comes before behavior. If you are going to accomplish any task, especially in the Lord's work, you must first set your mind to do it. What you believe you can do, you are far more likely to do it. If you believe you cannot do it, you probably won't even try.

Nehemiah had told the people about the deplorable condition of the wall surrounding the city of Jerusalem. He had surveyed and sized up the scope of the job. He had secured the necessary resources and had set before the people in the simplest terms what was needed to get the job done.

There were three crucial factors (according to the record) which made for fruitful results. The first crucial factor was the people. These were not individuals with independent interests, but were a faith fellowship of persons who believed collectively in the power, provisions, and promises of God.

The second crucial factor was the work. Because the people were a congregation, they were willing to do three types of work. The first type was creative work. They pooled all of their resources and ideas collectively to accomplish the task. The second type was concerted work; they worked as one. The third type was constructive work. Nehemiah placed different workers at different spots to do various jobs.

The third and perhaps the most crucial factor was the mind. The word mind consisted of one's will, one's heart, one's innermost thought and desires. The people did not just say, "Okay let us do the work", they believed in their innermost being that the work the Lord had given to their hands to do could be done.

Thus Nehemiah is careful to put it in the record—*"So we build the wall, and the entire wall was joined together up to half of its height for the people had a mind to work."*

Pray with me while I talk from this all important subject <u>"Having A Mind To Do The Lord's Work"</u>.

To have the mind; to keep the mind to do the Lord's work; there are some things believers must do. I shall mention a few.

I.   **Have The Supplies For The Struggle**

First, to keep a mind to do the Lord's work, you must make sure that you have the supplies for the struggle.

Nehemiah's King had given him a passport with his signature on it. This was necessary as he traveled from one province to the other back to Jerusalem. Nehemiah not only had a passport with the King's signature on it, the King sent with him the captain of the army and horsemen. The bottom line is—the builder had the King's blessings.

I don't know how you feel about it, but I think I need to tell us it is a struggle to live what we call the Christian Life. There is a struggle my brother; there is a struggle my sister in being a disciple of Jesus Christ.

It is only a little inconvenience to be a church member. All you have to do is show up every now and then for a worship service, put in a few dollars when you feel like it, and be a member in good standing with your church. But, if you are going to be a genuine born again Christian—spirit filled—washed in the blood of the Lamb—you are going to have to live your faith; put into practice your profession, and that is going to take everything in our very being by the power of the Holy Spirit to do what God wants you to do.

These people did a great work for the Lord. They kept a mind to do the Lord's work because they had the necessary supplies for the struggle.

II.   **Realize That Trouble And Opposition Will Come**

Another thing that helped these people to keep a mind to do the Lord's work was the realization that trouble and opposition would come. The Bible says that when Sanballat and Tobiah heard about the work that was being done, it grieved them exceedingly that there had come a man to seek the welfare of Israel.

I want you to get the picture here. Nehemiah and his group traveled between 750–900 miles—no problem; he leaves his job, gets days off from work—no problem; he crosses rivers—no problem; crosses provinces—no problem; no enemy attacks him. He tells the people what God had laid on his heart to do and the folk respond to what he said—no problem. They strengthen themselves for the job before them—no problem.

But then we read that Sanballat the Horonite, and Tobiah the Ammonite, and Geshem the Arabian heard about it, laughed them to scorn, and even despised them. In other words, you could see fire in their eyes; cussing on their lips; and contempt in their hearts.

I need to tell somebody this day when you are living the Christian life, you must realize that opposition and trouble will come. I tell young ministers all the time—don't you think just because you have a burning zeal to preach God's word in your heart that you are God's anointed and appointed, commissioned, consecrated, and committed that everybody will love you. There will be some folk whose bell you won't ring. Somebody will get mad at the good you do; somebody will hate your guts.

So, one thing that will aid a people in keeping a mind to do the Lord's work is a realization that opposition and trouble is going to come.

III. Realize The Need For Each Other

Another thing that caused these people to have a mind to do the Lord's work was their realization of their need for each other.

On this journey through this life, we must realize our needfulness of others. Nehemiah made no effort to be a solo performer. He gathered about him a crew to assist him in doing the work.

I'm amazed at the number of people I meet daily who foolishly think that they got it altogether enough to make it by themselves. We are living in an *"I", "Me",* and *"My"* generation. There are folk in the body of Christ who think and live like that. But to maintain a mind to do the Lord's work, we must realize our needfulness of others.

IV. Commit The Work To The Lord

One more thing I must mention. To have a mind to do the Lord's work, one must reckon the work and commit that work to the Lord.

Any work that is of God has no reason to fail. When the critics and opposition came against Nehemiah, he said to them—"We are going to build this wall; not merely because I'm leading the movement, it is the God of heaven who will prosper us an we, His servants, are going to stay on this wall until the job is finished and our victory is won."

When you get burdened down and troubles come in your life, and you don't know which way to go, stop looking at your problems; stop counting your doubts. Start looking to the hills from whence cometh your help. There is no telling what God can do if you only believe.

Everywhere I go, everywhere I look, I see or hear a testimony that God is still running this business. Every breath of air, every ray of light, every raindrop and flake of snow declares that God is. Every disease that is cured, every sin that is forgiven, every soul that is saved, and every miracle of grace declares that God is.

If God did not exist—

- Birds would not fly;

- Fish would not swim;
- Flowers would not bloom;
- Rivers would not flow;
- Grass would not grow;
- And we would not be.

Ours is an all-powerful God. He speaks and it happens. He commands and it is done.

CHAPTER IX

"But rise, and stand upon thy feet; for I have appeared unto thee for this purpose, to make thee a minister and a witness...."

Acts 26:16

He had moved to Tulsa. He had become the Assistant Pastor of Mt. Zion. He had been acknowledged and accepted in the community and the district. Now it was time for George Calvin McCutchen to journey to the Oklahoma Baptist State Convention, which meets the third week of October each year.

In 1952 the convention met at Mt. Zion Baptist Church, Tulsa. As is custom with the Convention, the host pastor is programmed to preach the sermon for the opening session the following year. Following in this tradition, when the Oklahoma Baptist State Convention met at the historic Calvary Baptist Church in Oklahoma City during the third week of October 1953, Reverend J. H. Dotson's name appeared on the program to preach the opening sermon.

Reverend Dotson, being ill and not being able to continue most of his pastoral duties, requested that his new assistant, the Reverend George Calvin McCutchen, be allowed to stand in his place. Dr. E. W. Perry, President of the Convention, agreed and young McCutchen made his first appearance before the Oklahoma Baptist State Convention.

Reverend Dotson also asked that Reverend McCutchen be allowed to serve on the Finance Committee, a position Reverend Dotson had served for many years. This arrangement was accepted and Reverend McCutchen served on the Finance Committee with Dr. J. P. Potter, Rev. M. D. Johnson, and Mrs. Levicia Johnson.

In 1978, he was elected to serve as Vice President-at-Large under the Presidency of Dr. E. Jennings Perry. McCutchen served in this position for four years. Because of the tenure clause of the State constitution, Reverend McCutchen was forced to move up or move out. He lost the 1982 election to Dr. T. Oscar Chappelle, Sr., and for the next four years Doctor McCutchen worked and served in any capacity of the convention that he was asked.

In 1986 President Chappelle broke the tenure of the State Convention and was elected to serve another four years as President. Dr. McCutchen was elected to serve once again as Vice President-at-Large.

Dr. Chappelle passed in April 1990, and Doctor McCutchen completed his obligation and served out Dr. Chappelle's unexpired term. During the 93rd session of the State Convention which convened at the Bethlehem Baptist Church, Lawton, Oklahoma October 24, 1990, Dr. G. Calvin McCutchen, Sr. was elected to serve as President of the Oklahoma Missionary Baptist State Convention.

President McCutchen spent many hours visiting District meetings throughout the State and helping Pastors in what ever way he could to help better their cause in serving Christ's churches. During the 100th Anniversary of First Baptist Church, Chickasha on November 11, 1993, this leader was honored by the declaration of "*McCutchen Day in Chickasha*".

He has been honored to be the speaker for many occasions, including the Banquet speaker of the Oklahoma Progressive Baptist Convention. He was the speaker at Revival meetings all across the State; taught study courses and gave lectures where ever he was asked; because no church was too large or too small for President McCutchen to give his attention.

In 1994 President McCutchen was again honored when the City of Guthrie, Oklahoma presented him with the Key to the City. He received two Keys to the City of Ardmore, Oklahoma—one in 1991 and again in 1994. He was again honored for outstanding services to the Western Regional Youth Conference, when they met in Tulsa in April 1997.

This young country boy, *One Of The Whosoevers*—George Calvin McCutchen—stopped by the State Convention in 1953. He made an outstanding statement and placed his mark; and continues to be a dedicated leader and a true servant of God and his people.

HEAVEN'S MEASUREMENT OF A PREACHER'S SUCCESS
Scripture II Corinthians 3:5-9; Job 16:19

"Not that we are sufficient of ourselves to think anything of ourselves, but our sufficiency is in God."

II Corinthians 3:5

The miraculous power which the Creator has given to everyone, including the gospel preacher, is the desire to succeed. No matter what career or profession one may choose, there is generally a list of requirements that must be recognized and adhered to, if we are to become successful in it.

Seldom, if ever, does anybody ever accomplish anything worthy of recognition by chance. For most of us, if we can claim any degree of success we obtained, required and even demanded blood, sweat, tears, and maybe a lots more. Life in the gospel ministry, contrary to what most people think, is more struggle than ease. We spend far more time climbing mountains than we spend resting in the valleys. The cross, instead of a cushion, is the symbol of our faith, and no one knows this better than the gospel preacher.

In this success oriented society in which we live questions often asked are—Who is the successful preacher? How do you measure success in the gospel ministry? Three methods of measuring success are often used.

The first of these measures of success is the *Bottom Line Approach.* This is basically the approach used by businesses. The bottom line definition of success goes strictly by numbers. Are the figures better this year than they were last year in terms of membership size, amount of salary, and the number of staff.

The second measurement of success is by *Personal Satisfaction*. We ask how satisfied have we been with ourselves and our ministry; have we given our best to God and his people.

The third measure of success is the *Spiritual Approach*. This standard is not measured in results, but in our faithfulness to God. Paul says it better than myself when he wrote—*"Not that we are sufficient of ourselves to think anything of ourselves, but our sufficiency is in God."*

Pray with me while I talk from this all important subject—<u>How God Measures Our Success</u>. I think I need to tell us, according to God's word, our standard of success can never be based on one another or on our own accomplishments. I am definitely of the opinion that the true success of the preacher is often measured by the wrong yardsticks. The Apostle Paul makes this observation—*"Not that we are sufficient of ourselves to think anything of ourselves, but our sufficiency is in God."*

I.   **Not By Earthly Goods or Material Possessions**

Let me say first of all, God does not measure a preacher's success by his earthly goods or his material possessions.

Some folk tend to measure the preacher's success by the neighborhood and type of house he lives in, or by the make and model of car he drives. It's a good thing to live in a decent home and it's good to drive a good automobile, but this is not Heaven's yardstick for a preacher's success.

We preachers worry about this a good deal. There was a time I though I had arrived when I pooled a few resources and purchased that first Lincoln car. Now my goal is to trade it for a Grand Jeep Cherokee.

The Spirit has already condemned me in this—we preachers are often as vain as some of our members. We spend a lot of money for things we don't really need, to impress folk we don't really like. There was a time when I was not ready to attend a National Convention until I had purchased at least one new pair of shoes. The reason—I knew that so many preachers get very little out of a meeting because they spend most of their time on the outside watching one another's shoes.

We are to be more Christ like. Jesus knew poverty and misery at his own doors. Those of us who set such a high premium upon comfort and conveniences should remember that Jesus walked the dusty roads of Palestine and he himself said *"The birds of the air have nests, the foxes have holes, but the Son of Man hath not a place to lay his head."*

God's measurement of a preacher's success is not by his earthly god or his material passions.

II. Not By Degrees Earned Or Received

Secondly I think I need to tell us that Heaven don't measure a preacher's success by the number of degrees he has earned or received.

We must admit that this age in which we live demands that a preacher must know something. In any field of work, education is to make you better. The gospel preacher, of necessity, must be in the know about his people and his work. He ought to be learning more and more everyday.

It's a wonderful thing to hold a few degrees. I have a few myself (five to be exact), but I didn't become somebody the day I received a few degrees. I've known some preachers with as many degrees as a thermometer, without an ounce of preaching ability and very little common sense. And, we who stand in awe before folk of scholastic achievement and honors need to remember that Jesus never held a degree; He may not have finished high school; but Heaven registers His ministry a *Big Success*. So, I do not believe God measures a preacher's success by the degrees he holds.

III. Other Erroneous Yardsticks

Let me cite quickly a few more erroneous yardsticks for a preacher's success. Somebody needs to tell us that Heaven's measurement of a preacher's success is not by the size of his congregation; not by the salary he draws; and not by the number of offices he holds on the District, State or National level.

Let me move toward a conclusion here and share with us what I believe to be Heaven's yardstick for measuring the preacher's success. Let me ask you right now to pray with me while I talk. If you can't or won't pray, I'm going to ask you to pull up a chair and listen.

God measures our success by our faithfulness to him. He who is all sufficient makes us sufficient for the task. God only ask for the consecration of our lives; the dedication of our talents; and the faithful use of every opportunity to render service in His name.

Harriet Beecher Stowe wrote "<u>Uncle Tom's Cabin</u>"; 300,000 copies were sold in America in one year. This novel of fiction was ranked as one of the greatest achievements of the human mind, yet Harriet Beecher Stowe refused to take any credit for what she had written. She said, "I, the author of <u>Uncle Tom's Cabin</u>, no indeed. I could not control the story, it wrote itself. The Lord wrote it. I was but the humblest instrument in his hands."

It was so with Paul. He never conceived of himself as being adequate for any task. He never did anything alone; he had to do it with God.

We work in the strength of God; we lean on his everlasting arms. He has given us the right to lean on him and, when we come to the end of our days, He won't look us over for honors, but for scars.

Billy Graham once said we will gain the victory a few moments before sunset or sundown, but we will have all eternity to celebrate.

There is a reward for faithfulness. My witness is in glory and my record will be there. One day I will receive my crown.

HAVING FAITH IN THE GOD WE SERVE
Scripture: Isaiah 41:10; Proverbs 3:5-6

"Fear not for I am with you; be not dismayed for I am your God. I will strengthen you, yes, I will help you. I will uphold you with My righteous right hand."

Isaiah 41:10

"Trust in the Lord with all your heart, and lean not on your own understanding. In all your ways acknowledge Him and He shall direct your paths."

Proverbs 3:5-6

The God that we serve is the giver of every good and perfect gift—including His peace, His companionship, His help and His strength. As believers, as members of His church and friends of the cause of Christ, we are challenged in the sacred scriptures to embrace faith instead of fear. Fear and faith aren't good companions.

Fear is the child of doubt; faith is born of God. Fear generally ends in failure; faith generally leads to victory and success.

There are two hidden negatives church folk should constantly guard against. They are fear and dismay. As we move forward into an unknown future don't look back, don't focus on past failures. Such will cause one to become fearful, and it will add to one's dismay. Acknowledge your past failures, but don't dwell upon them.

Looking within also might add to one's dismay. When we lean on our own understanding, this is harmful to one's faith. So I've stopped by here on my way to heaven just to say—as we move out into the New Year, don't look back; don't look around you; and don't spend too much time looking within.

Looking within can also be depressing unless there is a Devine examination of one's self. May I challenge you to keep looking up? May I challenge you to <u>**Have Faith In The God We Serve**</u>"?

Although we may not be able to see faith, hear faith, nor smell faith—yet faith can move mountains; can calm raging seas; conquer hostile enemies; open blinded eyes; and win spiritual victories. The Lord is saying to you this day—*"Fear not, I'm with you; be not dismayed for I am your God. I will strengthen you and help you; I will uphold you with my righteous right hand."*

A very wise man also left this challenge in the word of God—*"Trust in the Lord with all your heart and lean not on your own understanding. In all your ways acknowledge Him, and He shall direct thy paths."*

Pray with me while I talk from this all important subject—"<u>**Have Faith In The God We Serve**</u>". There are many reasons I urge you to do this. However, I shall mention but three and I'm through.

1. We should have faith in the God we serve because of who He is.

2. He fills the entire universe with His presence.
3. Nobody is above Him or like Him. He is always, was, and forever will be.

I. Because Of Who He Is

I challenge us to have faith in the God we serve because of who He is. Everything testifies to the fact that He does exist. Atheists may deny it; unbelievers my ignore it; and the heathen may not recognize it, but that doesn't change anything—God is.

Everything testifies to the existence of God. Every star that twinkles declares it. Every spade of dirt, every ray of light, every breath of air—yes, every flake of snow and every disease that is cured is a miracle of God's grace.

If God did not exist the birds could not fly, the fish could not swim, the flowers could not bloom, the rivers could not flow, and the sun could not shine. And furthermore, if God did not exist there would be no solutions to our problems, no answers to our questions, no freedom to enjoy, and no future to look forward to. We need to have faith in the God we serve because of who He is.

II. He Fills The Entire Universe With His Presence

One can see His glory everywhere, and one can feel His touch everywhere. All power belongs to Him. He speaks and it happens; He commands and it is done; He rules the rulers; He judges the judges; He controls the controllers. Nothing is done on earth or in heaven but what He is keenly aware of.

This includes every wind that blows, every bird that sings, every flower that blooms, every dog that barks, every raindrop that falls, every thought that enters one's brain and mind, every word that is spoken and every beat of everyone's heart.

He fills the entire universe with His presence. He designed the universe and all of its wonders. He positioned the stars in their places. He ignited the blaze of the sun. He established the earth with its land and seas. He put oxygen in the air we breathe. He taught fish to swim and birds to sing. He fills the universe with His awesome presence.

You can have faith in the God we serve. He's the God who—

- Brought plaques upon Egypt and Pharaoh;
- That divided the Red Sea for Moses;
- That shook down the walls of Jericho for Joshua;
- That conquered the giant Goliath for David;
- And He is the God who helped Noah survive the universal flood.

We can have faith in this God we serve because He fills the entire universe with His awesome presence.

III. Nobody is Above Him Or Like Him

Finally, we can have faith in the God we serve because nobody is above Him or like Him. He always was, He is, and He will always be. He is above all and beyond all.

He is the supreme authority over everything and everybody. He sees all, hears all and knows all. He knows all the answers. He has all the solutions. He knows every individual. He sees everything and He speaks every language.

He specializes in making the impossible to be possible. He's good at making saints out of sinners. He is good at making leaders out of loafers. He makes believers out of unbelievers. He makes friends out of enemies. He's good at making loyalists out of betrayers. He can make victors out of victims. He always was—He is—and He will always be.

He can take the corrupt and make them pure. He can take liars and make them truthful. He can take the rude and make them kind. And above all, He can take the bad and make them good.

We can trust this God we serve. He can wash your sins away. He can give you unspeakable joy. He can give you blessed assurance, everlasting life and a hope of heaven. He can move mighty mountains. He can scatter our worse fears. He can mend broken relationships.

He is a great fixer. He can fix absolutely anything and everything, and I might ought to tell you that whatever He fixes stays fixed. On the morning of creation He painted the sky blue, and through the ages the paint has never cracked or peeled. From the day He put the stars in their silver sockets, none have been sent out for repairs. Whatever He fixes—stays fixed.

In closing I'm going to ask you to have faith in the God we serve because it is He who—

- Helps us pay our bills;
- Open doors of opportunity'
- Provides wisdom for adverse situations;
- Gives us peace in the midst of our storms;

It is He who provides—

- Food for our tables;
- Vehicles for us to drive;
- Shoes for us to wear;
- A house for us to live in;
- Health for us to enjoy; and
- A song for us to sing.

And, to prove to ourselves; to show to a sin cursed world; and to make it up to Him, we ought to stand on His promises, place our lives in His hands, allow Him to direct our steps, serve Him with all our ability, and love Him with all our hearts.

THE NEED FOR THE FOURTH MAN
Scripture: Daniel 3:24-26

"Then King Nebuchadnezzar was very surprised and jumped to his feet. He asked the men who advised him 'Didn't we tie up only three men? Didn't we throw them into the fire?' They answered, 'Yes our king.' "The king said, 'Look! I see four men. They are walking around in the fire. They are not tied up and they are not burned. The fourth man looks like the son of the God'."

Daniel 3:24-25

No lies are worse than lies in religion. To substitute things material for things spiritual is a terrible sin. Folk who have no faith in a materialistic, unholy god should not be required to worship it. And furthermore, the Holy, all-wise, all-seeing and all-powerful God we serve deserves and demands that we worship Him with a pure and undivided heart.

In this scripture the Devine Spirit has prompted me to talk from today concerns Nebuchadnezzar, the King of Babylon, who made an image of gold. It was 120 feet high and almost 12 feet wide. He set his image up in the plain of Dura. He invited all of his leaders throughout his kingdom to come to its dedication. All who came for the festive occasion were told when and how they were to worship the image the king had set up. They were further told that all who did not fall down and worship this image would be cast in the midst of a fiery furnace.

On the day of the dedication, folk were there from everywhere. The king was so pleased to see acres of people bowing at his command, worshipping his materialistic hand-made god. But his contentment did not last very long.

He observed that far out in the knelling crowd there was a strange disturbance. There were three young men (Hebrew) he had exalted to high positions of leadership, who were actually standing while all the others were bowing down. The king questioned them about their behavior.

There reply was—*"We know full well the penalty we must pay for our disobedience—but, oh King, it's all about God and not about us. We will not be guilty of stooping at standing time. The God we serve is truly able to deliver us. And, even if He decided not to do so, let the record show we will worship the Lord our God. He only will we serve."*

Upon hearing their bold statements and observing the rash decision they had made, angrily the king ordered the furnace to be heated seven times hotter. Fully clothed, these three men were bound and cast into the flames. By the time their bodies should have been reduced to ashes, the king came down and personally conducted an investigation concerning the results.

He was amazed, surprised, even confused. He said to his servants— "Didn't we cast three men in?" They said, "Indeed we did." "Weren't they bound?" Their response was—"They were." "Then come here—see for yourself. I see four men loose in that furnace and the fourth one looks like the Son of the God."

From this familiar Bible story we learn another great Bible secret—**It's All About God, Not About Us.** Pray with me as I use the remaining moments to discuss—"<u>Our Need For The Fourth Man</u>".

I.   **Contempt For Religion And The Church**

Note first of all, many folk are saying that there is no need for the fourth man by their contempt for religion and the church. All around us folk are plunging headlong into eternity without a thought of their need for the fourth man.

They seem to be doing all right today, but they refuse to think about tomorrow and what it might bring. During the yesteryears we sang—*If you trust and never doubt, He will surely bring you out."*

The problem many folk have today is they have more doubts than faith. Doubt causes one to feel that nothing can help, or will help, or change the situation. Doubt denies the existence of a God who can. Doubt takes the devil at his word. It believes every thing the devil suggests. What faith reaches out for—doubt moves it farther away.

A person in this day and age can get fifteen cents above breakfast money, and be found stooping at standing time—by their contempt for the church and any form of religion. The truth of the matter is they think they can make it all by themselves.

II. **He Demands Full Surrender**

Another reason many feel that there is no need for the fourth man is that He demands full surrender.

I think I need to tell somebody today that it is not easy to live a meaningful, genuine Christian life. Being identified, being loyal to the fourth man means forsaking many worldly pleasures and full surrender to Him.

Being identified with this fourth man challenges the choice we make. It forces one to choose one's friends, one's life style—what we do, where we go, how we live, even what we believe. Many feel there is no need for the fourth man because He demands full surrender.

III. Our Need For The Fourth Man

In this third and final thought of this message, I call our attention to the evidence supporting our need for the fourth man. There is evidence in the sacred scripture supporting our need for this fourth man. The Bible says, *"In Him we live and move and have our being."* Jesus himself said, *"Without me, ye can do nothing."*

We also have historical evidence supporting our need for the fourth man. We see His footprints in the sands of the centuries. Empires have risen, fallen, and are now forgotten because their leaders failed to consider their need for the fourth man.

We need the fourth man because He makes possible every worthwhile achievement. Paul realized this when he put it into the record—*"I can do all things through Christ who strengthens me."*

The power of this fourth man is inexhaustible. He pours His power into the heart of every believer. He can be both here and there at the same time. His touch is inspiring; His ears are attentive; His love is unfathomable; His grace is unbelievable; His mercy is everlasting; His power is unlimited; His joy is unspeakable; His help is so reliable; His promises are dependable and He is faithful in all and to all.

This fourth man has everything everybody needs.

- If you have a problem—He has the solution.
- If you have a question—He has the answer.
- If you have a disease—He has the cure.
- If you have a crisis—He has the needed miracle.
- If you have a thorn in your flesh—He has sufficient grace.

Whatever you need, the fourth man has it. He can do whatever needs to be done. If you need deliverance from drugs or alcohol—He can do it. If you need an attitude adjustment—the fourth man can do it. If you just need a friend—He is a friend that sticks closer than a brother.

Having someone in charge of our lives is not enough; we need someone capable in charge. That is why we need the fourth man.

Because of that fourth man these three Hebrew men were able to walk from that fiery furnace without a single hair on their head singed, nor their clothing burned, not even the smell of fire on their garments.

I close with this—as believers we need, at all times, to know we are already in a spiritual warfare. It is a battle between the forces of evil and the forces of good. It is impossible to resist the devil with our own strength; if we do attempt it on our own, our strength will become completely exhausted.

The key to resisting Satan is to force him to deal with the one who lives in our hearts. When the devil knocks at the door of my heart and asks who lives there, the dear Lord Jesus goes to the door and says George C. McCutchen, Sr. used to live here, but he moved out. Now I live here.

The devil seeing the nail prints in the hand and the pierced side, immediately takes flight and leaves me along. It would be a mighty fine thing if every life and every home had Jesus in residence.

THE NEED TO TURN AROUND
Scripture: Proverbs 14:12; Matthew 7:13-14

"There is a way that seems right to man, but its end is the way of death."

Proverbs 14:12

"Enter by the narrow gate for wide is the gate and broad is the way that leads to destruction, and there are many who go in by it. Because narrow is the gate, and difficult is the way which leads to life, and there are few who find it."

Matthew 7:13-14

Allow me to introduce this message by sharing an experience that was ours while traveling from Tulsa to Hammond, Louisiana for a visit with my wife's parents who liver there.

It was during a rainy season. Because it had rained so much in the states, some of the roads were covered with water; some rivers had reached flood stage, causing some familiar highways to be rendered unsafe to travel. Somewhere between Alexandria and Baton Rouge, we saw a sign in bold red letters—ALL THROUGH TRAFFIC TO BATON ROUGE—TAKE HIGHWAY 51—BRIDGE FOR HIGHWAY 71 IS BEING REPLACED.

Not being too familiar with one road or the other, the sign meant very little to us, so we kept on Highway 71—the usual, familiar road we had always traveled. It is possible that we traveled 20 to 25 miles before we were confronted with a rude awakening and a very serious problem. Had it not been for a strong barricade in the road, we would have plunged headlong into a swollen river.

The sign on the barricade read—"**If you are troubled as to what to do now, I suggest that you go on back to where you saw that Detour Sign.**"

It is very easy to make the wrong turn while you are driving and, unless you turn around, you will never arrive at your desired destination. Going the wrong direction will cost you both time and money and, the further you travel the wrong direction, the more it will cost you.

Although you may regret having made the wrong turn, it will do you no good to simply regret it—you must turn around. And although you may come up with an abundance of excuses for having turned the wrong way, excuses will never substitute for not turning around. You can blame others for your mistake, but that will not replace the need to turn around.

Many centuries ago a very wise man made the observation "*There is a way that seems right to man, but its end is the way of death*". Jesus, in His Sermon on the Mount, shared this same idea with His followers. He said, "*Enter by the narrow gate, for wide is the gate and broad is the way that leads to destruction; and there are many who go in by it. Because narrow is the gate and difficult is the way which leads to life, and there are few who find it.*"

Many there are who are headed in the wrong direction. They are headed on one of the many dead-end roads, and they don't know the peril they are in. Hence, there is the need to turn around—and the sooner the better for them. That is what this message is about today—"**The Need To Turn Around**".

Three things I'm going to say about this and I'm through.

I.   **A Fatal Frustrating Confusing And Aggravating Experience**

I think you will agree with me when I say that going in the wrong direction can be a fatal, frustrating, confusing and aggravating experience. A lot of negative things can happen to you when you are headed in the wrong direction.

You could arrive, like I did, at a washed out bridge; you could run out of fuel before you arrive where you want to go; and, if you are not careful, you might end up missing the event you intended to attend. Have you ever stopped to consider that?

- Adam and Eve should have turned around but they didn't, so they were cast out of the Garden of Eden.
- Lot and his family needed to turn around but they didn't, and they ended up in the wicked cities of Sodom and Gomorrah.
- Pharaoh and his army needed to turn around but they didn't and they ended up drowned by the Red Sea.
- Samson needed to turn around but he didn't, so the Spirit of the Lord departed from him.
- Judas needed to turn around but he didn't, so he betrayed the Lord and went out and hung himself.
- Ananias and Sapphira needed to turn around but they didn't, and as a result of their lies, both dropped dead at the Apostle's feet.

Going in the wrong direction can be a fatal, frustrating, confusing and an aggravating experience.

II.   **No Good End To An Evil Path**

If you are on an evil path, you need to turn around because no one comes to a good end who selects and evil path. Apparently there are some who think that the road of dishonesty and deceit will get them to where they want to go, but it won't.

Apparently there are some who think the road to envy and jealously will get them to happiness and satisfaction, but it won't. Apparently there are some who think the road of anger and revenge will take them to a fulfilled life, but it won't.

Apparently there are those who think the road of laziness and indifference will carry them to eternal fulfillment, but it won't. And apparently there are those who think the road of verbal or physical abuse will give them respect from others, but it won't.

They will be greatly disappointed, for all these roads eventually end in heartache and utter despair; therefore, they need to turn around. No one comes to a good end who selects and evil path.

Listen to me. If you are traveling down the road of broken vows and commitment—you need to turn around. If you are traveling down the road of—

- Sensual lust and desires;
- Ungodly ignorance and foolishness;
- Greed and self-indulgence;
- Disobedience and lawlessness;
- Disrespect and rebellion; and
- Shame and disgrace

You need to turn around for no one comes to a good end who selects an evil path.

III. **Turn Around While You Can**

My final though is this—if you have gotten on the wrong road, and you know it, you need to turn around while you can. The longer you travel down these crooked, sinister, wicked, crowded and fatal roads, the more difficult it will be to turn around.

If you continue the wrong road you are traveling, you will discover the ruts of sin get deeper and deeper; the hills of depression will get steeper and steeper; the cliffs of vanity get higher and higher; the way of transgression gets harder and harder; the turn of events get yet sharper and sharper; and the ride of wickedness gets rougher and rougher. You need to turn around while you can.

Before I go to my seat, I might ought to say a word to the Saints. Up until now I've been talking mostly to sinners. Allow me to speak to the Saints. If you—

- Are not praying as much as you used to;
- Are not studying God's word as you should and ought to;
- Are not attending church as much as you used to;
- Are not worshipping the lord as much as you used to;
- Are not submissive to the Holy Spirit;
- Are not witnessing to others as you used to; then

You are going backward and not forward, and you need to turn around. I need to tell somebody today if you're not singing the songs of Zion like you used to; not giving from the heart like you used to; not enjoying the Lord's presence like you used to; not standing firm on the promises of God; not showing love to one another like you used to; not hungering and thirsting after righteousness as you used to; or not following in the footsteps of the Savior like you used to; then you are going backward—not forward—and you need to turn around.

SERVANTS NOT CELEBRITIES
Scripture: Mark 10:43-45

"... but whoever desires to become great among you shall be your servant. And whoever of you desires to be first shall be slave of all. For even the Son of Man did not come to be served, but to serve and to give His life a ransom for many."

Mark 10:43-45

As Christians we need to follow the example of Jesus and dedicate our lives to the service of our Lord. When there is work to be done for our Lord, oftimes we give only excuses—and an excuse is what one gives when they do not have a good reason.

When was the last time you heard someone say like Isaiah— *"Here am I Lord, send me"*? When there is some real service to be rendered in Jesus name (some real work to be done) more likely you will hear someone say,

"Get someone else; let George do it"—George meaning anyone else, but not me.

When many of us as Christians (church folk) come to the end of our earthly journey—when we are done with this world and the world is done with us—our lives will be one of many regrets.

We will regret that we did not serve Christ better; we did not love Him more; we did not speak of Him often to our unchurched and unsaved friends; and we will regret that we did not give more of our lives to the advancement of our Lord's Kingdom here on this earth.

Unfortunately, we live in a society that either do not know how to serve or does not want to serve. Many don't even know how to spell the word. Instead of spelling it—S E R V I C E, they spell it—S E R V E U S.

In this scripture the Lord has placed on my heart to talk from today, Jesus is telling His disciples that He is calling them to be servants and not celebrities. That was a very difficult lesson for the early disciples to learn, and it is a difficult lesson for us to learn too. The lesson we all need to learn is—**As Believers We Are Called To Be Servants, Not Celebrities**.

Jesus said, *"Whoever desires to be great among you shall be your servant and whoever of you desires to be first shall be slave of all. For even the Son of Man did not come to be served, but to serve and to give His life a ransom for many."*

Pray with me while I talk from this simple but important subject— "<u>Servants Not Celebrities</u>".

Three things I'm going to say and I'm through. My first thought is—

I. **Celebrities Prefer Sitting Above Serving**

Celebrities would desire to sit and be served. Celebrities desire high positions, sometimes they have low motives. We find this in the case study today.

Jesus was marching toward Jerusalem while His disciples lagged behind. In a short while Jesus would be handed over to the authorities and condemned to death; crucified upon an old rugged cross. James and John, His disciples "Sons of thunder", came to Jesus at this most crucial hour to make an unusual request. They said to Jesus, "Grant

us to sit, one on your right hand and one on the left, in your glory."
These two disciples had no idea what they were asking.

Jesus said to them—"You don't know what you are getting
yourself into fellows. Can you drink of the cup, I drink of? Can you
be baptized with the baptism I am baptized with?"

Quickly they answered—"We are able." In spite of their
enthusiasm, Jesus denied their request.

When the other ten disciples heard about this, Jesus called all of
His disciples together and told them—you and I are servants, not
celebrities. *"Whoever desires to become great among you shall be your
servant. And whoever of you desires to be first shall be slave of all. For
even the Son of Man did not come to be served, but to serve and to give
His life a ransom for many."*

Celebrities prefer sitting above serving.

My next thought is this—

II.   **God Can Use You Where You Are**

You don't have to be a star to be in God's show. You don't need
to read another scripture; you don't need to pray another prayer;
you don't need to repeat another creed or confession; you don't need
to attend another church service; you don't need to hear another
sermon preached—God can use you right were you are simply
because we are called to be "<u>**Servants Not Celebrities**</u>".

Let me tell you why I say this. God uses willing vessels, not
brimming vessels. When I check my Bible I observed that God
uses people from every walk of life. They are willing vessels, not
brimming vessels. He used—

- Matthew—a government employee, a tax collector. He became an Apostle.
- Gideon—a common laborer who became a valiant leader of men.
- Jacob—a deceiver whose name was changed to Israel.
- Deborah—a housewife who became a judge.
- Moses—a stutterer who became a deliverer of the people of God.

- Jeremiah—a child who fearlessly spoke the Word of the Lord.
- Aaron—a servant who became God's spokesman for Moses.
- Nicodemus—a Pharisee who became a defender of the faith.
- David—a shepherd boy who became a giant slayer and later a king.
- Hosea—a marital failure who prophesied to save Israel.
- Joseph—a prisoner who became Prime Minister.
- Abraham—a Nomad who became father of many nations.

There was Peter, the business man who became the rock on which Christ built His church. God can use you right where you are. He uses willing vessels more than brimming vessels. We are called to be "<u>Servants Not Celebrities</u>".

My final thought is this—

III. All God Needs Is You—All Of You

Our service to the Lord must be personal.

- Mary, an unknown virgin, gave birth to the Son of God, the Savior of the world.
- Nehemiah, a cup-bearer for his king, was used by God to rebuild the broken down walls around Jerusalem.
- Hezekiah, the son of an idolatrous father, became a king renowned for doing that which was right in the sight of God.

Albert Schweitzer said, "One thing I know, the only ones who will be really happy are those who will have sought and found how to serve."

Be an authentic servant of our God. They give anonymously, generously, voluntarily and personally. Authentic servants forget their past failure and move on with renewed determination.

CHAPTER X

"Go ye therefore, and teach all nations, baptizing them
in the name of the Father and of the Son and of the Holy
Ghost. Teaching them to observe all things whatsoever.
I have commanded you: and, lo, I am with you always,
even unto the end of the world. Amen.

Matthew 28:19-20

Young George Calvin McCutchen made his first appearance at the National Congress in 1949, when he went to the meeting in Memphis, Tennessee with Reverend L. Nelson of Ripley, Tennessee. After he came to Tulsa, Reverend Dotson allowed George to go in his place to the 1953 National Baptist Convention being held in Denver, Colorado.

> *"I arrived there by bus, without a reservation. I was fortunate to share a hotel room with a friend I met while walking from hotel to hotel trying to find a room."*

He started his work in the Congress of Christian Education as a guest lecturer in different divisions, on assigned subjects given by the Dean. He delivered the Inspirational Address to the assembly in Denver in 1962, and the Congress Sermon in St. Louis during the 1996 meeting.

George was first placed in the position of coordinator of the Youth Division, and later became Supervisor. When the Youth Department grew larger, the Dean decided to divide the Youth from the Youth Leaders. George decided to remain with the leaders, and for the past 25 years has served as Supervisor of the Young People's Leaders Division.

> *"I consider myself to be more of a Special Occasional Speaker than an Evangelist. But, I have been honored to preach in some of the greatest churches in this nation, for some of God's best preachers."*

During the past 50 plus years, George Calvin McCutchen, Sr. has conducted revivals and given lecture courses; preached installation sermons for Pastors, Anniversaries for Pastors and Churches; and has been the guest speaker for Men's Days, Women's Days, Missionary Days, Youth Days, etc., etc., etc., throughout Tulsa and the surrounding area, and the Nation. He is probably the only African-American Baptist Preacher to preach at a Catholic worship service. This he did in 1996 for Father Geir at the Christ The King Catholic Church in Tulsa.

He has lectured and preached in the Oklahoma City area for St. John Missionary Baptist Church, First Baptist Church Hicks Addition, St. Luke Baptist Church—Spenser, Oklahoma, Faith Memorial Baptist Church, New Zion Baptist Church, Unity Baptist Church, and St. James Baptist Church—Spenser.

George McCutchen conducted his first revival across the nation at the Mt. Pleasant Baptist Church in Belmont, North Carolina. Reverend Dennis Epting, Pastor and long time seminary classmate, invited him to return for five years in succession to run the annual revival meetings.

Through the years Dr. McCutchen has conducted revivals, evangelistic, stewardship, and leadership meetings at the Mt. Zion Baptist Church, Baltimore, Maryland; Grace Baptist Church, Mt. Vernon, New York (an annual speaking engagement for many years); New Bethel Baptist Church, Detroit Michigan; Hopewell Baptist Church, Hartford, Connecticut; New Spirit Baptist Church, Santa Ana, California; Portland Memorial Baptist Church, Louisville, Kentucky; and Emmanuel Baptist Church, Winston Salem, North Carolina.

During the 1970's and 1980's Pastor McCutchen would take his choir and as many members that would go (usually 2 bus loads) on a weekend trip to preach in churches around the United States. He and his church has traveled to such places as Pine Bluff, Arkansas; Dallas, Texas; Houston, Texas; Shreveport, Louisiana; DeMoines, Iowa; Memphis, Tennessee; Nashville, Tennessee; Wichita, Kansas; Bowling Green, Kentucky; and his home church in Rockfield, Kentucky where he preached before a standing room only crowd that had come to see their *"home boy"* who had accomplished much in his work for his Master.

George McCutchen's first Evangelistic Crusade was in 1963, when he traveled with a group of Southern Baptist Pastors to Jamaica British West Indies. One of the three Blacks among ninety Whites, George was assigned a church in Bunker's Hill, in the Falmouth area near Montego Bay. He preached there three weeks and more than 50 converts were credited to his preaching.

The next preaching experience abroad was ten years later in 1973. He participated in *Preaching Mission III*, sponsored by the Foreign Mission Board of the National Baptist Convention USA, Inc. Sixteen African-American Pastors went on a thirty day preaching tour of Africa.

"This was a very educational tour. We visited most of the mission stations supported by our Foreign Mission's Board."

His roommate and preaching companion was the late Dr. Samuel Austin, pastor of Grace Baptist Church, Mr. Vernon, New York. They arrived in Monrovia West Africa and journeyed to East Africa where they visited Kenya; then on to Blautyre, Mabwai, and finished the tour in Swaziland, the last country in South Africa.

Two years later, in 1975, Dr. McCutchen went on a tour of the Holy Land where he visited Caesarea, Philippi, Mars Hill, Bethlehem, Jerusalem, Jericho, and Bethany.

"I preached in Jericho, and in the Upper Room on Mount Zion. I walked where Jesus walked—visited Mt. Calvary and the empty tomb."

He has made several trips to the Bahamas, and has preached in several churches there. In 1980, Dr. McCutchen participated in a preaching mission with a group of Southern Baptist preaching in the Philippines.

Dr. George Calvin McCutchen, Sr., *One Of The Whosoevers*, stopped by this nation where he made an impression and received several awards and plaques including one for Outstanding Service from the Chaplain's Division, Fort Bliss, Texas (in 1985, he conducted a revival on base for service men and their families); and the Good Shepherd Award from the Indian Nation Council of the Boy Scouts of America.

A FOOL ON A MULE IN THE MIDDLE OF THE ROAD
Scripture: Numbers 22:1-31

"Then the Angel of the Lord moved on ahead and stood in a narrow place where there was no room to turn either to the right or to the left. And when the ass saw the Angel of the Lord, she lay down under Balaam, and he was angry and beat her with a staff."

Numbers 22:26-27

The term *fool* is very commonly used in the English language. A *fool*, according to the English dictionary is a person lacking in understanding; one destitute of commonsense; one who is unwise.

The term *fool* is found in the Bible about 150 times, describing a person's character and conduct. A person without spiritual wisdom, whose character is sinful, according to the sacred scriptures could well be called a *fool*.

It is no light matter to call a man a fool or for anyone to be called a fool. Even so, the Biblical character I have selected to talk about today has been termed by the more sensational preachers as the most unusual fool mentioned in the Bible. He has been called, and rightly so, "A Fool On A Mule In The Middle Of The Road".

Let me begin this message by saying that it is possible for anyone, at any given time, to act or play the role of a fool. But, this man, the Spirit leads me to talk about today, is a most unusual fool for several reasons.

I.   **Here is a man who was a fool, and there was no real cause for him to be.**

   The man's name is Balaam. He was a man of many noble qualities. He had a brilliant mind (and a good mind is a terrible thing to waste); he had many tokens of divine favor; he was a greatly gifted prophet of God; he was a man of strong convictions; he possessed an amazing knowledge of God; and he seemed eager in his search for divine guidance.

As a prophet of God, he had signed a pledge to speak the truth as he saw it. But we find him, on this occasion, doing his best to keep himself from seeing the truth. And he finds himself in a peculiar predicament—a fool with no reason to be. He can well be termed, as we shall later discuss, as—"A Fool On A Mule In The Middle Of The Road".

II.   Secondly, he was not an uncommon kind of fool.

This I say, because he tried to take God along with him in his foolishness. He asked God not to know what was right, but to grant him the opportunity to do what he knew to be the wrong.

The nation of Israel had won many battles because they had allowed the Lord to fight their battles for them. Balak, the King of the Moabites who had become fearful of Israel's many victories, hit upon the idea of getting a sorcerer to curse them and so weaken them that he could use his army to drive them out of the land.

Balaam, God's prophet was recommended for the job. They came and made him an offer of money that he couldn't easily refuse. He had gained a reputation for putting a hex on folk, but never in his life had he dared to curse anyone who God had blessed. Instead of telling that King's messengers to get lost, he saw a chance for popularity and personal gain. He told them to let him talk to God about it. He knew that God wouldn't go along with him in such foolishness, so on the next day he informed them that it was contrary to the wishes of the Lord, and sent them on their way.

A few weeks later a delegation of more prominent men came and offered him an even larger monetary reward. He told them that he would go back to God and see if He wouldn't change his mind. Here's where he made his terrible mistake. He wanted the glory and the honor; he could use and really wanted the money; and he wants to please himself without displeasing God.

He struggles between his convictions and his corruption. He knew what was right, but he begs God's permission to do wrong. He was not an uncommon kind of fool. He tried to take God along with him in his foolishness. The result is he ends up—"<u>A Fool On A Mule In The Middle Of The Road</u>".

III. He Lied To Himself

Another reason he is seen as a fool—he got caught on the most dangerous form of lying—he lied to himself. He told himself God wanted him to go because God didn't strike him dead when he put a blanket and a saddle on his mule and started on his self-determined way.

I think I need to tell us here that God will not force anyone, either you or I, to walk in the pathway of duty. But, he has all kinds of ways to make you wish you had. If a man lack the blessings that come from God, it is impossible for him to succeed. God will give you just enough rope to break your own neck. My Bible says, *"The way of the transgressor is hard."*

Balaam got caught in the worse form of lying, he lied to himself. He convinced himself that what he knew was wrong would be perfectly alright, and he ends up "<u>A Fool On A Mule In The Middle Of The Road</u>".

IV. He Failed To Use Good Sense

He is a most unusual, but not too uncommon fool, in that he failed to use good sense in a world of nonsense. He thinks he is wiser than his mule.

A mule is better able to take care of himself, better than any other animal. Let me explain. A mule is more sure footed; a mule know how to save his strength. You can't make a mule do more than he wants to do.

I think I need to tell us, one must learn to use good sense and common sense in a world of nonsense, or be willing to suffer the consequences and pay the price.

God was angry with Balaam, but because of his love for him, sent an Angel to stand in his way to keep him from destruction. Balaam thinks he's smarter than his mule, but his mule can see more than he does. The mule saw the Angel with his sword drawn and became unmanageable. He tried to keep this mule in the middle of the road, but his mule turns out of the road into the open field. He whips the mule back to the road, but the mule runs into a wall and crushes his master's foot. By this time they came to a narrow place where they can't go to the right or to the left. The mule sees the Angel of death again and falls beneath the rider. He thinks he's smarter than his mule, but he finds himself talking to his mule and his mule talking to him.

God opens his eyes and he sees what the mule saw all the time. He also sees himself as "<u>A Fool On A Mule In The Middle Of The Road</u>".

I have to close this message, but I dare not do so without sharing what I believe to be the message God intended for us. **First**, I should remind us—it is bad to play the role of a fool when you have no real reason so to be, and you can't take God with you into your foolishness. Use good sense and common sense in a world of nonsense.

Secondly: Expect any kind of ill accident to happen when you willfully stray from the pathway of duty onto the wrong road. Never hesitate when trying to tell Satan no. Tell him to get behind you and in the name of Jesus, don't push.

Thirdly: God is with us when we are right, and He is also with us when we are wrong to get us right.

ARE YOU PREPARED TO GIVE UP YOUR ISAAC
Scripture: Genesis 11:1-2

"And it came to pass after these things, that God did tempt Abraham, and said unto him, Abraham; and he said, behold, here I am. And he said, take now thy son, thine only son Isaac, whom thou lovest, and get thee into the land of Moriah; and offer him there for a burnt offering upon one of the mountains which I will tell thee of.

Genesis 22:1-2

Perhaps you have already reacted and responded to my question by saying, "I don't have a son named Isaac." I know that fact as well as you do, yet I must in all fairness inform you that all of us have some kind of Isaac in our lives. Therefore, before you tune me completely out I'm going to ask everybody under the sound of my voice to engage in a moment of silent reflection. I'm going to ask you to ask yourself "What is my most precious earthly possession? What is it upon this earth that I treasure more than anything else in the whole world? What person is there in my life which would leave me void if he or she was no longer around."

There is without a doubt an Isaac in your life. It may be your husband whose name is Bob, Ed, or Bill, but if he is your most precious treasure, he is your Isaac. It may be your wife whose name is Mary, Louise, Katherine, or Ann, but if you love her more than you love anything or anyone else in the world, she is your Isaac.

Your Isaac may be your mother, your father, sister or brother, your children or grandchildren, or even one of your very close friends. And furthermore, your Isaac may not be a person at all. Your Isaac may be your job, your position, your title, your bank account, your wardrobe, your car, your good looks, your influences or even your bad habits, or your unconfessed sin.

And my question is—if God put you to the test and told you that the only way you could prove your love for him would be to give up your Isaac, would you be willing to do it. So now I 'm back to the subject the Divine Spirit has prompted me to speak from today—<u>Are You Prepared To Give Up Your Isaac</u>.

There are three truths I'm going to ask you to think on and if possible agree with me about—and I'm through.

I.   **God Sometimes Gives His Servants Strange Orders**

First, let's agree on this first lesson—God sometimes gives his servants some strange orders. In terms of human wisdom, God may give you some orders that don't make any sense. We find as we study the Bible, God has given his servants some strange orders.

One day God told Noah to build an ark so that he and his family could be saved from a flood. Noah had never seen an ark and he had seen very little rain, yet God tells him to prepare for a flood. He is to build something which there was no model of, to protect himself from something he had never heard of—some strange orders.

Then one day God gave Moses a strange order. He told Moses to go way down in Egypt land and tell old Pharaoh to "let my people go".

Think about this. Here was Moses—a fugitive from justice, a man wanted for murder who had been on the run for 40 years, whose only weapon is a stick—yet, he is told to go to the commander and chief of the world's largest and best equipped army and say to him "God told me to tell you to let my people go"—strange orders.

In our text today God give Abraham some strange orders. God said to Abraham, "Take with you your only son—yes Isaac, whom you love so much. Go to the land of Moriah and sacrifice him there as a burnt offering."

Mind you, this was the son Sarah had when she was almost 90 and Abraham was 100 years old. He was a child God had given to them in keeping of a promise. Isaac was truly a wanted child, yet God said to Abraham I want you to take this child, your son, up to Mt. Moriah and offer him a sacrifice to me. Sometimes God give to his servants some strange orders.

This brings me to the next thought:

II. Do As God Has Commanded

Abraham, this grand old man of faith, without knowing all the answers proceeded to do just as God had commanded. Abraham's faith was put to its ultimate test. He took his son, Isaac, to Mt. Moriah and, as he was preparing the altar with his son looking on, Isaac spoke up. Isaac had seen his father sacrifice animals on previous occasions. Isaac noticed something was missing, so he spoke up saying, "We have the wood, the flint to make the fire, the altar is all prepared, but where is the lamb for the sacrifice?"

Abraham, still not knowing what God was going to do answered and said, "Son, God will provide. I don't understand what He's doing and I don't know when He's going to do it. All I know is that the Lord will provide."

I'm sure there have been times in your life, as well as mine, when our backs were against the wall and we didn't know which way to turn, but there was something deep down inside saying—The Lord Will Provide. It may have been a bill that was over due, your creditor was giving you a hard time and you didn't know where the money was coming from, but your faith went into action and something deep inside said—The Lord Will Provide.

Our fore parents survived on only a fraction of what we have today. You ask me how they did it. I believe that every day they made it on the strength of those words—The Lord Will Provide.

A lot can be said about the faith of Isaac. Abraham took him, bound his hands and feet, even placed him on the altar. He then took his knife and drew it back and was about to thrust it into Isaac's chest when one of God's angels cried out from Heaven saying—Abraham, don't take your son's life; you passed your examination; you have passed the faith test and the obedience test; you have proved to God that you were willing to give him your most precious possession.

Abraham then looked and saw a ram which had been caught by his horn in the bushes. Abraham, the grand old man of faith, without knowing all the answers proceeds to do just as the Lord commanded.

This brings me to the final thought which is this:

III. God Wants A Living Sacrifice

God didn't want Isaac's dead body as a sacrifice, God wanted Abraham's living sacrifice. God knew that unless Abraham was willing to give up his most precious possession in the person of Isaac, he wasn't willing to give himself totally in God's service. So, when Abraham showed his willingness to give up his most precious possession, Isaac, he became eligible to work on God's staff and reap all the benefits which accompanied the job.

So, let me close with my initial question—<u>Are You Prepared To Give Up Your Isaac</u>. God don't want a dead child placed on the altar, God wants you—a living sacrifice—your reasonable service.

He wants not a part of you, but all of you. He wants your legs to walk for him. He wants your tongue to talk for him. He wants your eyes to see for him. He wants your ears to hear for him. He wants your voice to sing for him. He wants your mouth to witness for him.

He wants your legs to run errands for someone languished upon a bed of affliction. He wants your hands to reach down and lift some weary traveler who has fallen by the way. He wants your heart to reach out to the lost, the last, and the least of all that need to be told about the love of God.

THE KIND OF SERVICE OUR LORD COMMANDS
Scripture: Matthew 25:1-46

"His Lord said to him 'Well done, good and faithful servant; you were faithful over a few things, I will make you ruler over many things. Enter into the joy of the Lord'."

Matthew 23:21

Those of us who have trusted Christ as our personal Savior, and have submitted ourselves to His Lordship, and have made a vow to do God's work God's way, in His will, on God's timetable and for His glory—expect one day to be commended by our Lord.

I don't know about you but, when I come to the end of my up and down experiences on this earth, I expect to be commended for a job that was not merely done—I want to hear Him say **WELL DONE**.

In illustrating what the Kingdom of Heaven is like, Jesus told this parable where he taught a great and vital truth about faithfulness. Jesus stressed that it is absolutely essential for His servants to be totally faithful in all matters and, as a result of being faithful there were wonderful, blessed benefits and rewards.

Nothing can substitute for faithfulness. I believe God wants us to be faithful. He especially wants us to be faithful to Him. Without faithfulness one's faith becomes weak, one's possibilities will become limited, one's reputation will become ruined, one's testimony will become empty, and you have no one to blame but yourself.

I don't read anywhere in the scriptures that God offers any rewards for unfaithfulness. And, if He is going to say "well done thou good and faithful servant", it will be because it was well done and it cannot be done well unless you are faithful.

The Devine Spirit has lain on my heart to talk today about "<u>The Kind Of Services Our Lord Commends</u>". The text reads—"*His Lord said to him 'well done good and faithful servant. You were faithful over a few things, I will make you ruler over many things. Enter into the joy of the Lord"*.

Three things I'm going to say about this and I'm through.

I.   **God Commends Thoughtful Service**

First I think I need to tell us that God commends thoughtful service. There is a need for wisdom in serving God. A good deal of trouble has been caused in the world by too much intelligence and too little wisdom. Someone has said, and I fully agree—"A fool tells what he will do, a boaster tells what he has done, a wise man does it and says nothing."

A fool is quick to say, "I can't"—a wise man says, "I'll try." From the errors of others a wise man corrects his own errors.

Matthew quotes the Master as saying—"*Who then is a faithful and wise servant, whom the Lord hath made ruler over his household, to give them meat in due season? Blessed is he that servant whom his Lord, when He cometh, shall find him so doing.*" (Matthew 24:45-46)

Our Lord commands thoughtful service.

II.   **Our Lord Commends Thorough Service**

Can I also tell you that our Lord commends thorough service? Service for the Master is not to be disorganized and haphazard. On the contrary, it is to be efficiently and thoroughly planned. Paul writes to the church at Corinth—"*Let all things be done decently and in order.*" (I Corinthians 14:40).

And God not only expects us to be faithful, He requires it. He is a jealous God and requires our total allegiance. He expects us to be loyal, trustworthy, faithful servants. He commends thorough service.

He expects us to keep our word to others. He expects us to attend church on a regular basis. He expects us to—

- Read our Bibles and pray;
- Give offerings and pay tithes;
- Fulfill duties and responsibilities; and
- He expects us to apply God's principles to our everyday lives.

Our Lord will commend thorough service.

III. God Will Commend Tireless Service

Then it goes without saying—God will commend tireless service. The Bible says, *"Happy is that servant whom his Lord, when He cometh, shall find so doing."*

The Savior condemns loafers and time-wasters. He himself was a tireless worker. He is reported as saying, *"I must work the work of Him that sent me while it is day, the night cometh when no man can work."*

Listen to me. Not everybody—

- Has the ability to be a physician
- Has the education to be a teacher
- Has the talent to be a gospel singer
- Has the knowledge to be a lawyer
- Has the training to be a counselor
- Has the intelligence to be a scientist; or
- Has the calling to be a Minister of the Gospel

But, everybody can be faithful. Our Lord commends tireless workers.

Let me further explain who the tireless worker is. He or she is the one that didn't give up when the job became difficult to do; who didn't quit when others failed to help or encourage; who didn't get upset when things didn't go as planned; who didn't delay until a more convenient time or season; who didn't complain or grumble about what all was involved.

God knows whether you are really sincere in what you are doing, or if it's just a pretense. God knows whether you have done your very best, or if you've done just enough to get by. God knows whether you are doing it because you want to, or because you feel obligated to do it. And God knows whether you have done it unto Him, or only for personal gain.

These words as I close—each of us has been given talents by the King. The Holy Spirit distributes spiritual gifts according to the needs of the church. No one is left empty-handed. Each one has been given a gift. We can double our talents by our faithfulness. We can improve our own usefulness and fruitfulness.

Someone has said—one note is a sound; add some other notes and you have a song. One color, no matter how beautiful, is monotonous; add other colors and you have a cathedral window.

The ultimate reward for our faithfulness is the Lord's approval and praise. All of us would like to hear Him say, "Well Done". Let's use what God has given to us that we might bring glory to Him and that He might be glorified in us.

EVERYBODY HAS AN EMPTY SLEEVE
Scripture: Ephesians 4:15-32

"Put away from you all bitterness and wrath and anger and wrangling, and slander, together with all malice, and be kind to one another, tender hearted, forgiving one another, as God in Christ has forgiven you."

Ephesians 4:31-32

Some years ago I heard a story that changed my life by changing the way I look at other people. The story was about a stern, strict English teacher who ran his one room schoolhouse with an iron hand. "To spare the rod was to spoil the child," was his motto.

He was tough and demanding—a harsh disciplinarian. In that classroom he was the law—the prosecutor, the judge and the jury. The students were required to obey his rules submissively, or else they would reap the hard consequences for their actions.

One day a new student moved to town and joined the class at mid-term. He was given a seat at the back of the room. The school master decided to make an example of his stern rules to this new student. His idea was to show him, and to remind all the other children, that he was the absolute authority in that place. So he went to this new student and said, "Young man, you are new here, so let me explain to you how we do things in this classroom. I make the rules and you obey them. When I call on you to recite, I want you to stand on the left side of the desk, say your name loudly, hold your textbook in your right hand, and then recite. Do you understand?"

"But Sir", said the student.

"Don't you question me:, said the schoolmaster. "Just do it like I say and we will get along just fine."

Later in the day the schoolmaster did call on the new student. The boy stood on the left side of his desk as he had been told; he said his name loudly, so far so good; but he held his textbook in his left hand instead of his right.

This infuriated the teacher—thinking that the young man was defying him, he ran up to the student shouting, "Don't you disobey me. I told you to hold your textbook in your right hand."

The schoolmaster then grabbed the student, shook him harshly, and shoved him down in the seat. As the student fell back down into his seat, an empty sleeve swung around, revealing the fact that his young man had no right had to hold his book in. He had no right arm.

The point is obvious—and it is so important to remember: **everybody has an empty sleeve of some kind, and more often than not, we can't see it.**

It is so tempting to be harsh and judgmental of people when they don't do and act just like we want them to do. It is easy to be critical of others—to find fault—to point the finger. But, if we recognize that everybody has an empty sleeve of some kind, it is easier to accept other people, respect them, love them and allow your heart to go out to them.

How can you and I ever know the difficulties and burdens hidden away in the lives of the persons around us? Remember—"<u>Everybody Has An Empty Sleeve</u>.

That is why Paul's words in our text are so crucial. In these captivating words, Paul gives us his ethical punch line—*"Put away from you all bitterness and wrath and anger and wrangling and slander, and be kind to one another, tender hearted, forgiving one another as God in Christ has forgiven you."*

To sum it up in one sentence, in effect Paul is saying—treat other people as Jesus Christ has treated you, in the spirit of amazing grace. Why? Because everybody has an empty sleeve. If you can remember that, you will find it much easier to relate to others as you make your way through this world.

Three things I'm going to say about this and I'm through.

I.   **If You Know It's Easier To Forgive**

First, if you know about the empty sleeve, it is easier to forgive others. Every heart has secret sorrows and secret fears, secret burdens and secret regrets. Sometimes we think a person is cold and indifferent, when actually he or she may be deeply sad.

During my early days in the ministry I misjudged a lot of people because I didn't know their pains and I found it difficult to accept them. I recall an experience that was mine during my seminary days.

I was hired by a Methodist preacher to fill his pulpit in a small town outside Nashville. I would ride the bus and arrive there in time for Sunday School. I would sometimes give the Sunday review, or listen to the Director who was an excellent Bible teacher.

One thing I didn't like about him—when he finished Sunday School, he disappeared. I thought he just didn't want to hear me preach. I spoke to one of the other stewards about this. He didn't tell me why he did this; he offered to take me after dinner to the man's house and allow me to talk with him or find out the reason for his actions.

He took me to the man's house. The man literally had an empty sleeve. In that home there was child with MS. He and his wife could not ever leave him alone. He, being the Director of Sunday School, was allowed to come and fulfill his duty; but was to hasten home and allow his wife, the child's mother, to attend church.

We never know what problems are hidden away in some folk's lives. Realizing they might have an empty sleeve, this will help you to become more sensitive and more forgiving. If you know about the empty sleeve, it's easier to forgive others.

II. **If You Know It Is Easier To Understand**

If you know about the empty sleeve, it is easier to understand others. I once knew a minister who hated to make hospital visits. Not because he resented being around folk who were ill, but because he hated elevators. When he went to visit, he would always take the stairs. If the patient was on the 14th floor—there would be 14 flights of stairs he had to climb.

Folk didn't understand this. It was his empty sleeve. He got claustrophobic when he rode elevators. He could drive miles to visit friends and relatives in other cities, but he wouldn't dare take a bus or an airplane because of his fear of tight places.

When his friends, co-workers and family members knew this about him, it was easier for them to understand. If you know about the empty sleeve, it is easier to understand others.

III. **If you know It Is Easier To Love Others**

Finally, when you know about the empty sleeve, it is easier to love others.

Everybody has an empty sleeve of one kind or another and, if we realize that, it makes it easier to love. As you and I move out in the future, remember that it is to err on the side of grace, to cut other people some slack—forgiving one another as God in Christ has forgiven you. It is always best to live in the gracious spirit of Christ. God wants us, as believers, to live as we pray.

A poet put it like this—

I knelt to pray when the day was done
And prayed, O God bless everyone.
Lift from sorrowing hearts the pain,
And let the sick be well again.
And then I wake another day
And carelessly went on my way.
The whole day long I didn't try
To wipe a tear from any eye,
I didn't try to lift the load
From any brother on the road
I didn't even go to see
The sick man just next door to me.
And yet again when the day was done,
I prayed, O God bless everyone.
But as I prayed into my ear
There came a voice which whispered clear
Pause hypocrite before you pray
Whom have you tried to bless today?
Life's sweetest blessings always go
By hands who serve Him here below.
And then I hid my face and cried
Forgive me Lord for I have lied.
And let me live another day,
And I will live the way I pray.

WHAT DOES A PREACHER DO
Scripture: I Peter 1-10

"I beg you to take care of God's flock, His people you are
responsible for. Watch over it because you want to, not because
you are forced to do it. Do it because you are happy to serve, not

because you want money. Do not be like a ruler over people you are responsible for. Be good examples to them."

I Peter 5:2-3

Many ministers have entered the gospel ministry because it seemed as if it would be an easy job. After they got into the ministry, they soon found out that the task of the gospel minister is not nearly as easy as it looks. Some readily admitted that they had misread or mistook their calling. They also found themselves a job where they could make far more money and have fewer headaches.

The average church member does not know what it is like to be a Pastor—a Gospel Preacher. Can I tell you, the Pastor's job is a difficult one. His time is not his own, which means he is always on the job. He is sometimes a lawyer, often a social worker, sometimes an editor, a bit of a philosopher, an entertainer, a lecturer, a statesman, and he is the local representative for every relief movement in the land.

People come to see him and he goes to see people continually. He visits the sick, buries the dead, marries couples, and counsels with them after they are married.

He plans programs, appoints committees and oftentimes, does their work for them, and he spends a considerable amount of time keeping people out of each other's hair. Oftimes on Monday mornings some child—who doesn't know any better—who overheard their parent's conversation says to him, "What a job! Only one or at most two hours of work a week!"

Can I tell us that the Pastor's job is a very difficult one. Therefore, with the aid of the Devine Spirit, I shall use the remaining moments of time given to me to tell you what makes this job so unbearable to some.

I.   **Deals With People Who Know More Than He Does**

First, I think I need to tell you that one thing that makes the Pastor's job so unbearable—he has to deal with people who think they know more about his job than he does.

After several years in college and seminary and, after forty-eight years of pastoral experience, I too am confronted with people who have had no seminary or personal experience in the Lord's work, who know everything. At least they think they do. The problem is—they don't know what they don't know.

Preaching is no easy task. We are duty bound to preach with ease, with authority, with clarity, with power and hopeful to get positive results. Yet there are people in his congregation who think they know exactly how to preach and what to preach, which makes the minister's job difficult. There's something else—

II.   **Deal with People Who Cannot Be Motivated**

The Pastor has to deal with people who cannot be motivated. Some congregations are like the preacher who loved his congregation—preached good sermons—loved his wife and children—did everything right with one exception. At two in the afternoon, he would leave his office and was gone for one hour. Soon the parishioners became uneasy about this pastor's curious schedule and began to ask question.

They went to the deacons with their concerns—could the Pastor have a girl friend in a neighboring town? Unsure of what to do, they went to the denominational leader with their concerns. His district overseer approached him about his regular strange schedule.

He asked him to go for a ride with him as he kept his schedule. At 2:00 o'clock in the afternoon, they drove out to a high hill overlooking a small town and a railroad track that ran through the valley. After sitting there quietly for some time, a beautiful silver train streaked through that valley at a very high speed. He said to his Bishop—"Isn't that a beautiful sight?" The Bishop agreed.

He said, "This is where I come every afternoon. I come here to be inspired. It is the only thing moving around here that I don't have to push."

The Pastor learns from experience—If you don't push nothing moves. What makes the Pastor's job so difficult—he has to deal with people who cannot be motivated.

III. People Think The Word Of God Applies To Everyone But Them

The Pastor has to deal with people who think the Word of God applies to everyone else but not to them. People who come to hear the preacher preach should bring a spiritual shovel with them. As the preacher shovels it out, the members ought to be kind enough to shovel it in. But the average member comes to church with a gospel pitchfork. The preacher pitches some truth to them; they throw it off to someone else.

A frustrated preacher said one morning to his congregation—"Every one in this church is going to hell if they don't change their ways." One fellow in the rear of the building began to laugh. The Pastor went back where he was and asked him why he was laughing at the truth he had told? He answered, "Because I don't belong to this church."

I have said—the Pastor's job is a difficult one because in many cases the folk he is sent to serve help makes it so by

1.   Thinking they know more than the preacher does;
2.   By dealing with so many who cannot be motivated; and
3.   By dealing with so many folk who think the Word of God applies to everyone else, but not to them.

IV. The Job The Minister Is Called To Do

What does the scripture say about the job the minister is called to do? The text I read says—"*... the preacher is to feed the flock of God which He has made you responsible for.*"

The church does not belong to the preacher. It belongs to God. If a pastor stood up before a congregation and said—Today, when you make out check, make it out to me—all the people in the church would think he was crazy; rightly so. But some television ministers can tell millions to make their check out to him or her, and folk do it without reservation.

It's the Lord's flock. *The preacher's job is to feed the flock of God.*

He also is charged with the responsibility to *supervise the flock*, taking oversight thereof. Not by constraint, but willingly; not because he wants money, but because he is happy to serve.

I really have to close this message. May I do so by sharing these important words with you? They who honor the servant of God, honors God. He who honors God, God will honor. And God is on the side of everyone who honors Him. God calls for unselfish service.

And I need to tell you this—Satan does not want any of us to succeed in serving the Lord. Although I'm now cramming for the finals, my work on earth is nearly done and my race is nearly run. Can I tell you it pays to serve Jesus? It pays everyday; it pays every step of the way. I plan to run on and see what the end is going to be.

I do close with this. I was discharged from the Marines in 1946. I applied for enrollment in the American Baptist College in the fall of that year. This was mid-spring and until that time I had nothing meaningful to do. I applied for unemployment and I was told I could and should receive $20.00 a week for 52 weeks if I so desired.

I helped my sister around the house until I ran out of something to do. When I went to sign up for my next check, I told the employment office, "I'll take any job."

They sent me on a job to make $27.00 a week—I could have made $20.00 staying at home doing nothing. My day had told me—"One's bread is sweeter when he works for it."

That first job was at a restaurant at the airport. They were opening this new restaurant the next morning. We went to work at 5:00 a.m. and worked all night long—washing dishes, scrubbing floors, stocking the pantry, putting food in the freezer. We worked until daybreak.

The restaurant was to open at 8:00 a.m. A crew showed up to do the same—minus a dishwasher who was delayed until about noon. The man asked for a volunteer. Everybody had an excuse but me. I said to those fellows, "Although I've been here as long as you have, I'll stay. But take this number—my sister is worried about me by now. Tell her I'll be on after a while, but the man I work for has told me to work here a little while longer."

I think of the many ministers I know—some better by nature than I am by practice, have punched their time clocks and gone home. I'll be on after a while—but, the man I'm working for has asked me to work here a little while longer....

CHAPTER XI

"For God so loved the world, that He gave His only begotten Son, that <u>whosoever</u> believeth in Him should not perish, but have everlasting life.

John 3:16

Fifty-four years ago a young farm boy from the hills of Kentucky, who knew that he would be one of God's Whosoevers; a recent graduate from the American Baptist College of the Bible in Nashville, Tennessee got off a train in Tulsa, Oklahoma. He came to serve Mt. Zion as Assistant Pastor, but has done so much more than that for Mt. Zion, the Tulsa community and surrounding areas, the District, the State of Oklahoma, and the Nation.

After having served 50 years as Pastor of Mt. Zion Baptist Church, Tulsa, Oklahoma, on January 13, 2007, at an annual Church Business meeting, Dr. George Calvin McCutchen, Sr. read to the congregation his resignation letter as Pastor of Mt. Zion Baptist Church.

Pastor McCutchen is retiring from the Pastorate of Mt. Zion, but this leader, this teacher, this Kingdom builder will never retire from the gospel ministry nor from being one of God's faithful servants.

And so the story continues as George Calvin McCutchen, Sr. continues preaching God's word; and as he continues to consult with, counsel, mentor, and advise young ministers thru his Barnabus ministry.

Barnabus was an older, wiser, and seasoned minister who worked along aside the Apostle Paul as he established some of the New Testament Churches.

Dr, McCutchen believes that his fifty plus years of experience can be a valuable resource to the younger ministers in the area.

You see—*"the man I'm working for has asked me to work here a little while longer...."*

He states that if he had the opportunity to write on his tombstone, it would only be two words and they would be—"**I Tried**"

978-0-595-46452-4
0-595-46452-1

Printed in the United States
101733LV00001B/151-174/A

9 780595 464524